Sophie Michell

CHEF ON A DIET

EAT WELL, LOSE WEIGHT, LOOK GREAT

Photography by David Loftus

KYLE BOOKS

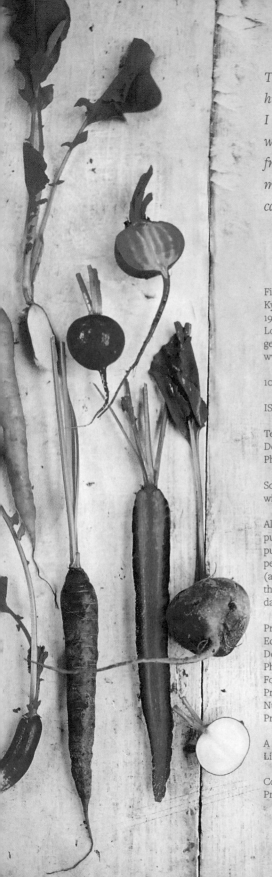

*This book is dedicated to my future
hubby, Eoin Clarke, mainly because
I love him very much, and because
when I see him a weight is lifted
from my shoulders – thank you
my love for supporting me and my
career so much.*

First published in Great Britain in 2016 by
Kyle Books, an imprint of Kyle Cathie Ltd
192–198 Vauxhall Bridge Road
London SW1V 1DX
general.enquiries@kylebooks.com
www.kylebooks.co.uk

10 9 8 7 6 5 4 3 2 1

ISBN 978 0 85783 349 5

Project Editor: Tara O'Sullivan
Editorial Assistant: Amberley Lowis
Designer: Heidi Baker
Photographer: David Loftus
Food Stylist: Julia Azzarello
Prop Stylist: Iris Bromet
Nutritional Analysis: Alina Tierney
Production: Nic Jones and Gemma John

A Cataloguing in Publication record for this title is available from the British
Library.

Colour reproduction by F1 London
Printed and bound in China by 1010 International Printing Ltd.

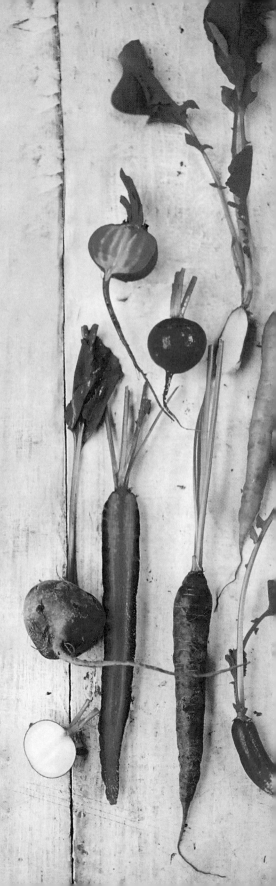

Contents

Introduction

'MY DOCTOR TOLD ME TO STOP HAVING INTIMATE DINNERS FOR FOUR. UNLESS THERE ARE THREE OTHER PEOPLE.' ~ *Orson Welles*

My weight has gone up and down for as long as I can remember. I was a chubby eleven-year-old, a super-skinny fourteen-year-old, a bloated twenty-year-old (working on a pastry section), a healthy twenty-three-year-old, a super-skinny twenty-six-year-old, a very plump thirty-year-old and finally an unfit, overweight thirty-three-year-old, with an ever-expanding stomach.

We have all heard the phrase 'never trust a skinny chef', and it is one I used to repeat to myself often, but, truthfully, after opening two restaurants and writing two books in as many years, my weight had got out of control. While I didn't need to be a skinny chef, I did want to be a healthy one. Everything about being a chef can go against healthy eating, from being surrounded by a range of tempting foods to the requirement to taste everything for flavouring, and I was desperate for a change. After being at Belgraves hotel for two years and feeling that the kitchen and team were settled, I wanted to take care of myself again. Then my fiancé proposed on Christmas Eve and, after seeing photos of myself at our engagement drinks, I knew it was time for me to slim down. I actually felt bad about myself, and, crazy though it may have been, I was feeling really sad and disempowered.

I had to admit that life had become a conveyor belt of food and I wasn't letting any of it pass untouched; there was the burger to make myself feel better at the end of a busy shift in the kitchen, the Bloody Mary (or two) at Sunday brunch, as it was my only day off, and then the 'I'm exhausted I need a boost' biscuits at 11am. I was making unhealthy choices every day without even realising. I became a chef so I could surround myself with food, but I didn't want to be eating unthinkingly, gaining weight and feeling depressed about it.

Before I go further, I have to make clear that I abhor the fact that women are pushed all the time to be unnaturally skinny and that this can often develop into self-loathing and low self esteem. I think it's disgusting that anyone should ever feel they have the right to comment on another person's weight.

As a female chef running a busy kitchen, thinking about my appearance can be difficult. Kitchens are hot, sweaty places, where you live on adrenaline and spend your time dressed in voluminous chefs' whites and crap chef shoes. Yet, when it comes to doing any media work, you are still immediately judged on your image. I have done masses of telly over the years and, even when I was size 10, I was periodically trolled on Twitter by people saying I was too fat to be on TV.

So it might sound as though I am putting myself in a strange position by writing a diet book, but the truth is that I know that a lot of women, like me, want to feel a bit slimmer and healthier and want to have the tools to do that. Women are bullied constantly by the media, by their peers and by themselves over their weight and it's damn unhealthy. We need to find our balance – and that became my mission.

So I looked back over my career, thinking about the times when I was at my healthiest, to try and see what I was doing differently then. I've never been into fad diets, but sometimes I just seemed to be getting it right – so what was the key?

'TELL ME WHAT YOU EAT, AND I WILL TELL YOU WHO YOU ARE.'

~ Jean Anthelme Brillat-Savarin

After a bit of navel gazing, I realised that the time that I had been at my optimum weight and felt healthiest coincided with the years I'd spent as a private chef. In this role, taste and visuals are paramount, but you can't do the old restaurant tricks of lacing everything with butter and cream, as the food is for everyday eating. I needed to return to the sort of meals I had been cooking then.

At the same time, I had grown tired of seeing uninspiring diet books written with nothing but weight loss in mind, without the food and flavour being properly thought through. It seemed like committing to a diet meant waving goodbye to loving food, which is a reason that so many diets fail. We all know that lentils, brown rice and mung beans are good for you, but they don't exactly set my taste buds on fire. Likewise, for someone who takes great pleasure in the art of cooking and preparing food, committing to plain grilled meat and steamed vegetables feels like a punishment. I decided to use my years of experience as a chef to make healthy recipes that are delicious to eat and enjoyable to prepare.

After a few long talks with my publisher, I opted not only to write a book of diet recipes, but also to follow the diet myself to prove it works. This is good and bad. Good; to be given the chance to develop my very own diet. Bad; because it really exposes me to scrutiny – and a few lifestyle changes!

Developing a diet whilst working as a chef wasn't always easy, and I haven't always been that strict (the odd chip and canapé have definitely passed my lips!), but overall I have stuck to it, and I am getting results – more than from any other diet I have done in the past 10 years.

The Nitty Gritty

So, how does it work?

This isn't a super quick fix diet (although if you have a high volume of sugar and wheat in your normal diet, the weight will come off quite fast, especially at first). I want this to be seen as a way of eating on a more permanent basis. So if you have an overkill of pasta and wine one evening on holiday, the next day just get back to the system – all is not lost. Don't just give up after one slip up.

Following a healthy diet is a lifestyle choice, and as such, it's not just about what you eat. I do recommend exercising too. When I took up this diet plan, I also did a few 30 minute sessions in the gym each week and as much walking as possible. The exercise really helps, mainly because it releases endorphins. If you are a habitual comfort eater or big drinker, the endorphins you get from exercise can replace the good feeling you might have been seeking from all the wrong sources.

Ultimately, it's very simple. I wanted this diet, and the book, to be about the food, not about rules. So, to explain it as simply as possible:

Breakfast should be made up of protein and complex carbohydrates.
Lunch and dinner should be made up of proteins and vegetables.
THAT'S IT.

You get your good, energy-boosting carbs in the morning and these, mixed with protein, will keep you fuller for longer. When I was growing up, it was unheard of in my family not to have a cooked breakfast. Whatever time your day started (and it was often at 5am) you would have a full hot breakfast, with both protein and carbs. Looking back, this was a really good grounding (minus the 20 cups of sugary tea). We were never hungry before lunch and we never snacked. Breakfast is the most important meal of the day and, if you eat well, it stops you grazing later.

Lunch and dinner should be made up of protein and only plant-based carbs. In my experience, protein and plant-based meals are easier to digest and you don't go to bed feeling full and bloated.

An important part of the diet is to cut out as much sugar as you can. Sugar is not good for you. It has zero nutrients and really plays havoc with the body. Cutting sugar out will work best if you start off going cold turkey (which I admit is difficult, as sugar is in everything), but stick to it for a couple of weeks and soon enough anything sugary will suddenly taste unnaturally sweet and you'll crave it less. It's akin to giving up smoking (believe me, I know – I have been both a heavy smoker and sugar addict at times in my life) and you need to get right off the stuff, to then be OK with re-introducing it. This means at the beginning of the diet I would only have one or two of the sweet breakfasts a week as, even though they are designed to be far healthier than the norm, they are still sweet.

You might be thinking that the above all sounds a tad boring and, if you are not sure about what constitutes proteins, carbs, and sugars, and don't have a private chef like me at hand, perhaps even a bit confusing. Once you dive in, though, you'll see that boring is the last thing this diet is. There is so much variety and choice, and it really is all about the food.

Snacking

I am the grazing queen. I love picking at food all day long and being a chef can make that a dangerous tendency. To successfully lose weight you do want to avoid snacking, but you also want to avoid being hungry, especially in the first month of dieting. So, if you feel peckish between meals, it's better to have something than feel hungry and miserable, and risking cracking and eating completely the wrong thing. Have a slice of ham, half an avocado, a small piece of cheese, some pickles, some celery or some nuts. Don't worry, the weight will still come off, and being too hungry is the enemy of losing weight. I have this argument with my fiancé, as he thinks that any snacking is bad – but he will sit there and eat 'healthy' cereal bars and drink sugary smoothies. And guess who's lost the weight...?

Anyway, I've added some healthy snacks (see pages 174–179), should you need them.

Diet like a chef

So many books contain diet 'recipes' that are super boring OR have amazing cheffy recipes that are unbelievably high in calories. This book uses professional chef skills to make the 'diet' food taste good. You will discover new ingredients and new cooking techniques that should stay with you for life.

When I started this diet, I took packed lunches in every day. My staff thought I was nuts, as I have access to the whole menu, but it was the only way to get control. Plus I avoided staff mealtimes, as it was just too easy for me to eat the piles of pasta, risotto and fried chicken that my team love to cook.

Planning your menus, and the cooking itself, is something to look forward to (see page 188 for some sample meal plans). Thinking about that EPIC brunch you will have at the weekend with the Big Sur Eggs Benedict (see page 46) and a Bloody Mary, or the incredible Sunday lunch of Rib of Roast Beef, with Caramelised Shallot Cream and Wild Mushrooms (see pages 116–117). Get excited about the amazing foods you can eat, rather than feeling hung up on what you can't. You will not only start feeling so much better for eating more healthily, you will also have an amazing arsenal of new dishes at hand.

The top ten food myths that f**k me off – and why they're wrong!

* **'Avocados are too high in calories to eat on a diet'** – They are high in calories, yes, but they're full of nature's finest fats. They make a great replacement for richer items like butter and creams.

* **'Low-fat products are better for you'** – Never choose low-fat versions! They're full of nasty chemicals and sugars to make them taste better.

* **'Red meat is bad for you'** – Fine, if you eat 32oz steaks on a regular basis, your gut won't thank you, but good-quality red meat eaten in small amounts *is* good for you.

* **'Sugar is better than sweeteners because it's natural'** – Sugar is natural when it's in a sugar cane in a field, not when it's in your cupboard in a bag. Nowadays many sweeteners, like stevia, come from more natural sources and they can help you to lose weight and regulate blood sugar levels.

* **'You have to completely avoid chocolate if you're dieting'** – If I am really craving something sweet on a diet, a small bar of dark chocolate is a life-saver. Good-quality dark chocolate (70 per cent cocoa solids and upwards) has less sugar and contains antioxidants.

* **'Nuts are too fattening to eat on a diet'** –Yes, nuts are high in fat, but these are good fats. They also contains masses of nutrients, so don't avoid them.

* **'You shouldn't eat too many eggs, they are really high in cholesterol'** – Yes, the yolks contain fat and cholesterol, but anyone who consumes any form of processed food at all should be much more worried about that. Eggs are a major part of a healthy diet.

* **'Fruit is healthy, you should eat as much as possible'** – Fresh, unprocessed, seasonal fruit is a good source of vitamins. But you know how fruit tastes sweet? That's the natural fruit sugars in it. Be careful, avoid most fruit juices, and pre-prepared fruit. Eat fruit with the skin on and try and eat seasonally.

* **'You should avoid salt at all costs'** – Yes, large amounts of salt are bad for you, but the body needs some salt and it is nature's own flavour enhancer.

* **'All liquids are the same as water and hydrate you just as much'** – No, they don't. Water really is good for your skin, hair, body, digestive system and weight. Stop messing around and just drink lots of water every day.

Choosing foods

When I wrote my first ever cookbook, I included ingredients like quinoa, miso paste, seaweed and even coconut oil. These ingredients may seem mainstream now, but boy, were they weird then. In the years since, we have had a healthy food revolution and it's brilliant that I can happily talk about these ingredients and use them all the time now.

To help you understand how the foods used in this book fall into the diet plan, I've put together the simple lists below: good-vibe foods and bad-vibe foods. Good vibes lead to good energy, and for me, that is what it boils down to. When I eat well I am happy, positive and full of energy. Good food = good vibes. Bad food = bad vibes.

Good-vibe foods
* Proteins (meat, fish, eggs, cheese, nuts, etc.)
* Complex carbs (rye bread, quinoa, spelt flour, brown rice etc.)
* Good fats (avocados, olive oil, coconut oil etc.)
* Vegetables and salads

Bad-vibe foods
* Refined carbs (white bread, white pasta, white rice, etc.)
* Sugar (cakes, biscuits, white and milk chocolate, alcohol, sugary drinks, etc.)
* Deep-fried food (self-explanatory!)

When I am trying to lose weight, I personally cut out wheat and gluten – I find they mess with my mojo. In the beginning I also cut down on alcohol, HUGELY. This is the bit that sucks, I admit. I am not saying you can never have a drink, but I am saying be conscious of it and cut it out as much as you can. There's more on this opposite.

'LET THEM EAT CAKE.' ~ *Said no skinny person ever (or Marie Antoinette, apparently)*

I'm not into calorie counting – if you focus on the numbers too much, it becomes almost meaningless. Theoretically, you could choose to eat 1,500 calories' worth of Mars bars each day and claim to be dieting because it's below the recommended daily amount of calories. You might even lose weight, but I can guarantee you'd feel terrible. In contrast, 2,000 calories a day of good-vibe veggies and proteins will make you look and feel fab. So a successful diet is not just about limiting calories – in fact, some of my dishes are relatively high in calories. It's about how the body digests food and how protein and fats keeps you fuller for longer.

The recipes in this book are all accompanied by nutritional analysis so you can get a better understanding of what you are eating. This does include calories, as many people find them a useful reference, but focus on the more detailed breakdown for each recipe and pay attention to the way the food makes you feel – for example, noticing that the recipes with high protein leave you feeling satisfied for longer. Plus, get used to looking at the carb content and the saturated fat content – you want those two babies lower. To be low-carb, I aimed to keep the carb content below 20g per 100g of food.

If it were possible, I would say never eat sugar and processed foods, but I know this is hard, so I have added some slightly healthier desserts and sweets, for when you really need them. Obviously, when you are starting off, it's better not to eat them at all. People talk about natural sugars versus refined sugars, but really, sugar is sugar. Natural sugars almost all behave in the same way as refined sugars, so still need to be avoided or cut down.

'I USED TO JOG, BUT THE ICE CUBES KEPT FALLING OUT OF MY GLASS' ~ *David Lee Roth*

I love a good drink, but alcohol plays havoc with blood sugar levels. It's not just the calories, but the fact that the following day usually becomes a tired, sugar-craving carb fest.

Drinking does play a big part in a foodie's life, though, and I think it would be sad to have to give it up forever. So, while you are trying to reach your optimum weight, consider the following:

* Drink as little as possible. Try to have one high-quality drink now and again (see right), and avoid binges.

* Look at what you are drinking. I swear if the government put nutritional information on bottles of wine, beer and spirits, a lot of us would think twice. Sorry guys, but on this plan, beer, cider, alcopops and sugary cocktails are out.

* Drink masses of water in between alcoholic drinks. This will lessen the hangover and walking corpse look of the following day and will also make you drink less booze in the first place.

And that's it. I hope you enjoy this book and get a lot out of it. It really has been a labour of love for me: it's the most personal book I have written and the one that most closely resembles my real day-to-day cooking. At first, I thought it would be hard to write recipes in line with a restricted diet, but in fact I could have written another 100 easily. I hope this means that you'll be inspired to experiment and come up with your own spin on some of the recipes. There's a whole host of marinades, spice mixes, dressings and sauces for you to mix and match on pages 180–183, so you can really get creative.

Enjoy – and let me know how it goes!
Sophie x

Here are some of my favourite low-sugar alcoholic drinks.

* **Skinny Bitch Cocktail** – If I am on an evening out I usually order this, as it's the lowest sugar alcoholic drink I can think of: vodka, soda water and a few wedges of lime. Squeeze the juice in, and chuck the rind in, too, for the aromatic oils that are present in citrus peel.

* **Deluxe Skinny Bitch** – as above, but with yuzu juice instead of lime. If you're making this at home, you can get yuzu juice online and in larger supermarkets. Yuzu tastes a bit like pink grapefruit crossed with bergamot crossed with lime.

* **Gin, pink grapefruit and soda.**

* **Vodka, fresh ginger, mint, lime and soda.**

* **Ultra Brut Champagne** – I know Champagne is expensive, but let's face it, everyone feels glamorous with a glass of fizz (and distinctly less so after too many). So stick to the mantra of buying well and drinking less. Just have the odd glass or two when you really have something to celebrate. Go for Ultra Brut, as it has less sugar. Laurent Perrier do a lovely one.

* **Single malt whisky on the rocks** (but only one).

* **Bloody Mary** – makes you feel full and has the added boost of tomatoes and chilli.

* **Bloody Bullshot** – like its naughty partner Mary (see above), this is vodka in a spicy broth tinted with Tabasco and Worcestershire sauce. Use bone broth to be extra warming.

★★★ *I've rated every recipe out of three – one for the easiest, and three for those that are a little more cheffy.*

*Quick
Breakfasts
and Slow
Brunches*

Avocado, mint and white grape smoothie

✶✶✶ Smoothies are a very popular breakfast choice, but to be honest, they are something I tend to steer clear of, as so often they are packed full of puréed bananas, added fruit sugars and dairy, none of which start my day off well. This is my diet-friendly version, a natural protein smoothie. The avocados give it a silky, luxurious texture and the almonds contribute good fats to keep you feeling fuller for longer. It is not a very sweet smoothie, but I like its clean mint and lime freshness.

1142 ENERGY KJ	276 ENERGY KCAL	7.1g PROTEIN	23.9g FAT	1.1g SATURATED FAT	8.5g CARBOHYDRATES	6.1g TOTAL SUGARS	1.3g FIBRE	0g SALT

SERVES 1

½ avocado, peeled and stoned

2 tablespoons whole unblanched
    almonds

a handful of white seedless grapes

a handful of mint

juice of ½ lime

1 teaspoon agave syrup (optional)

150ml still spring water

a handful of ice

This is so simple! Place all the ingredients in a blender – I use a Nutribullet, as it gets everything super smooth.

Blitz until really smooth and enjoy.

Sunshine juice

*** *Sunshine in a glass: sweet, lovely and full of orange hues, this will perk you up no end. This is a simple juice that will appeal to non-juicers. It has the classic orange hit, but with the addition of carrots and ginger. Ginger is fantastic for combating nausea and will help to settle an upset tummy.*

374 ENERGY KJ	89 ENERGY KCAL	1.3g PROTEIN	0.7g FAT	0.1g SATURATED FAT	20.6g CARBOHYDRATES	19.9g TOTAL SUGARS	4.6g FIBRE	0.1g SALT

SERVES 1

2 carrots

2 apples

thumb-sized piece of fresh ginger

Place all the ingredients in a juicer. Blitz until really smooth and enjoy.

Spicy tomato juice

*** *Bloody Marys are one of my all-time favourite drinks. Sadly, as I have mentioned, I do suggest giving up alcohol for a bit if you want to lose weight: it messes with your blood sugars, and adds cartloads of calories. On top of that, the next day you crave carbs and sugar, which can lead you to make the wrong choices with food. To try and allay any Bloody Mary cravings, I created this juice, which has a heady hit of spice and is also full of nutrients.*

639 ENERGY KJ	150 ENERGY KCAL	6.3g PROTEIN	2.4g FAT	0.7g SATURATED FAT	27.4g CARBOHYDRATES	27g TOTAL SUGARS	8.9g FIBRE	1.2g SALT

SERVES 2

600g ripe tomatoes

100g cucumber

100g red pepper, chopped

2 celery sticks

1 red chilli, deseeded

squeeze of lemon juice

dash of Tabasco sauce

1 teaspoon Worcestershire sauce

100ml still spring water

pinch of salt

As before, place all the ingredients in a juicer. Blitz until really smooth and enjoy – just imagine it has a double shot of Grey Goose in it!

Liver-cleansing detox juice

✱✱ I can't promise that this will completely cleanse your liver – that very much depends on how hard you have been hitting it! But according to many studies, beetroot helps the liver-detoxification process along, and it is full of antioxidants and vitamins. I love the epic purple colour of this juice, and it tastes amazing, too. Caution: if you are anything like me, do not drink while wearing a white shirt!

| 338 ENERGY KJ | 79 ENERGY KCAL | 2.8g PROTEIN | 0.5g FAT | 0g SATURATED FAT | 17g CARBOHYDRATES | 16.3g TOTAL SUGARS | 4.8g FIBRE | 0.4g SALT |

SERVES 1

4 medium raw beetroots, unpeeled

2 sprigs of mint

5 celery sticks

1 apple

squeeze of lemon juice

Simply place all the ingredients in a juicer and blitz until really smooth, then serve.

Popeye juice

✱✱ This is the most popular juice at my restaurant Pont St. It's seriously green and delivers a good hit of nutrients, but includes a bit of apple to sweeten it up. If you're a die-hard juicer, remove the apple and add a couple of celery sticks. Green juices have become rather mainstream now – you can pick them up ready-made in many high street chains. Be really careful, though, as many contain high-sugar ingredients or fructose. Better to make your own.

| 244 ENERGY KJ | 58 ENERGY KCAL | 2.9g PROTEIN | 0.9g FAT | 0.1g SATURATED FAT | 10g CARBOHYDRATES | 9.6g TOTAL SUGARS | 3.2g FIBRE | 0.2g SALT |

SERVES 1

12cm piece of cucumber

a large handful of curly kale

a large handful of spinach

1 apple

Simply place all the ingredients in a juicer and blitz until really smooth, then serve.

Cashew nut, cinnamon and vanilla nutshake

✳︎✳︎ Nutshakes are great because they seem like a creamy milkshake but are actually full of good fats and proteins. The cinnamon and vanilla give the illusion of sweetness – this combination always works. This recipe was inspired by a Plenish milk I tried once and loved. The nutshakes on this page are higher in calories than my juices, so I regard them as a complete breakfast. They do give a significant protein boost, too, so I often have them before a hard exercise session, adding a spoonful of maca powder.

2386 ENERGY KJ	576 ENERGY KCAL	17.7g PROTEIN	48.2g FAT	9.5g SATURATED FAT	18.1g CARBOHYDRATES	4.7g TOTAL SUGARS	3.2g FIBRE	1g SALT

SERVES 1

100g cashew nuts

½ teaspoon stevia

½ teaspoon ground cinnamon

½ teaspoon vanilla extract

pinch of salt

200ml still spring water

Place all the ingredients in a blender. Blitz until really smooth and enjoy.

Peanut butter, cocoa and vanilla nutshake

✳︎✳︎ This nutshake feels quite decadent, as the peanut butter adds a bit of naughtiness and the cacao nibs taste of chocolate, yet they're full of antioxidants. This is quite rich and I would personally have it only as a treat or for a healthier take on a milkshake for children.

1044 ENERGY KJ	252 ENERGY KCAL	9.5g PROTEIN	21.2g FAT	5.4g SATURATED FAT	5.5g CARBOHYDRATES	2.8g TOTAL SUGARS	2.4g FIBRE	0.4g SALT

SERVES 1

2 tablespoons peanut butter

1 teaspoon stevia

1 tablespoon cacao nibs

½ teaspoon vanilla extract

200ml still spring water

Place all the ingredients in a blender. Blitz until really smooth and enjoy.

Spelt, coconut and lime pancakes

★★☆ *Pancakes are a bit of an indulgence – technically even these ones are not to be eaten every day if you want to lose weight. However, making them with spelt and not loading them with sugar does mean they're much better for you and will sustain you for longer. When I used to eat pancakes for breakfast, my family and I would joke about the ensuing pancake rage that would kick in by 11am, when my blood sugars crashed and the grumps would set in. This sugar crash can happen to anyone, so if you do crave pancakes, make them like this and enjoy them all the more knowing that your mood won't plummet. Coconut syrup has a lower GI than sugar, and tastes amazing into the bargain.*

2249 ENERGY KJ	540 ENERGY KCAL	17.1g PROTEIN	27.7g FAT	20.6g SATURATED FAT	61.9g CARBOHYDRATES	15.9g TOTAL SUGARS	8.6g FIBRE	2.5g SALT

SERVES 4 (makes 8)

250g white spelt flour

4 teaspoons baking powder

50g desiccated coconut

pinch of salt

3 free-range eggs, beaten

325ml semi-skimmed milk

1 teaspoon vanilla extract

zest of ½ lime, plus lime wedges to
    serve (optional)

50g coconut oil

50ml coconut syrup, to serve

Mix all the dry ingredients together in a large bowl.

In a separate bowl, whisk together the eggs, milk, vanilla extract and lime zest, then pour slowly into the dry mix and whisk until smooth. Let the batter sit for 30 minutes.

When you're ready to cook the pancakes, gently heat a large non-stick frying pan.

When the pan is hot, add a touch of coconut oil followed by a ladleful of the batter. Cook on a medium heat for 5 minutes, then flip over and cook on the other side for 5 minutes. Repeat with the remaining batter, placing the cooked pancakes on a plate in a low oven while you cook the rest. Depending on the size of your pan, you might be able to cook more than one at a time.

Serve the pancakes with coconut syrup, and lime wedges, if you like.

Orange blossom, white peach and honey salad

★☆☆ This is a simple, deliciously scented salad that can only really be made during those summer months when white peaches are in season. The orange blossom water in this recipe makes the already fragrant fruit even more aromatic. The honey is a natural sweetener that also works beautifully with the other ingredients. Let the fruit sit and macerate for a bit, so that all the delicate layers of flavour come out and a lovely sauce is created.

| 727 ENERGY KJ | 174 ENERGY KCAL | 6.8g PROTEIN | 10.4g FAT | 6.8g SATURATED FAT | 12.4g CARBOHYDRATES | 12.1g TOTAL SUGARS | 2.4g FIBRE | 0.2g SALT |

SERVES 4

**2 white peaches, stoned and cut
into wedges**

200g raspberries

1 tablespoon runny honey

1 teaspoon orange blossom water

400g Greek yogurt

Place the peaches and raspberries in a bowl.

In a small jug, mix together the honey and orange blossom water, then sprinkle over the peaches and raspberries. Mix well and leave to macerate for 30 minutes.

Serve with the yogurt.

Pineapple, chilli and agave salad with Greek yogurt

✱✩✩ This salad really wakes you up! The chilli is very invigorating, and I think that's just what you need in the morning. In many countries you will find chilli and spices at breakfast, and it's a healthy habit to embrace, as it gets your body moving and all the senses going. I serve this with real Greek yogurt, as it's higher in protein than any other yogurt.

920 ENERGY KJ	220 ENERGY KCAL	7.2g PROTEIN	12.4g FAT	8.1g SATURATED FAT	20.8g CARBOHYDRATES	20.7g TOTAL SUGARS	1.6g FIBRE	1.2g SALT

SERVES 2

200g fresh pineapple flesh, diced

1 tablespoon torn mint leaves

1 tablespoon agave syrup

240g Greek yogurt

1 teaspoon chilli salt

Place the pineapple in a bowl and add the mint and agave syrup. Leave for 10 minutes so that the flavours can develop and mingle.

Top each serving with a big dollop of Greek yogurt and a sprinkling of chilli salt.

Top tip

In the evening, make yourself a frittata in little muffin tins. Then, in the morning, you can grab a couple from the fridge and take them with you for a protein-paced brekkie on the go! You'll find a recipe for an Avocado, Chicken and Jalapeño Frittata on page 53, but you can change the fillings to suit you.

Quinoa porridge with goji berries, almond milk and cinnamon

★☆☆ Quinoa is such a popular grain these days. I included a dish featuring quinoa in my first ever cookbook, back at a time when it wasn't well known as an ingredient. Now it's very much in fashion and you'll find it everywhere. Quinoa is a super grain, full of amino acids and proteins, and it's also great for people who can't eat wheat. This porridge is one of the bestsellers in my restaurant at Belgraves Hotel. People love the fact that it is unique and dairy-free, with a low level of sugars. We won a prize for one of our other porridges, too, a coconut, papyaya and mango version. Porridge is making a real comeback, and has come a long way since I used to eat it as a child with golden syrup and salt.

985 ENERGY KJ	236 ENERGY KCAL	8g PROTEIN	10.3g FAT	0.6g SATURATED FAT	25.8g CARBOHYDRATES	6.3g TOTAL SUGARS	3.4g FIBRE	0+g SALT

SERVES 4

300g cooked quinoa

400ml almond milk

2 tablespoons ground almonds

2 tablespoons goji berries

2 tablespoons agave syrup

1 teaspoon ground cinnamon

½ teaspoon vanilla extract

2 tablespoons flaked almonds,
    to serve

This one's very simple! Just place all the ingredients (except the flaked almonds) in a saucepan and stir to combine. Place over a medium heat and bring to the boil – this should take about 8 minutes.

Divide the porridge between four bowls and serve sprinkled with the flaked almonds.

Coconut chia breakfast pot

✱✱✱ *I adore chia seeds. Admittedly, when soaked they look a bit like frog spawn, but I kinda like that. Chia seeds remind me of the desserts you get in Asia, and they are full of nutrients. For this breakfast pot I add a touch of maca powder, a superfood powder that is a great replacement for coffee, as it gives you a powerful energy boost. Not only that, it has a toffee-like flavour that I love. Soaked chia seeds also carry other flavours well. I sometimes make this with almond milk and raspberries, or even apple juice and grated apples to make a chia Bircher muesli.*

1085 ENERGY KJ	260 ENERGY KCAL	5.7g PROTEIN	15.7g FAT	7.5g SATURATED FAT	27.4g CARBOHYDRATES	15.1g TOTAL SUGARS	15.9g FIBRE	0.1g SALT

SERVES 4

300ml coconut water

100ml coconut milk

1 teaspoon maca powder

50g sultanas

50g chia seeds

50g desiccated coconut

agave syrup, to serve (**optional**)

Mix the coconut water, coconut milk and maca powder together in a bowl, then add the sultanas and the chia seeds. Leave for 10 minutes, then stir well and divide between four bowls or glasses. Cover and pop in the fridge for a few hours. I sometimes do this the night before, but it only really needs a couple of hours.

When you are ready to eat, sprinkle with the desiccated coconut and some agave syrup (if needed) and enjoy!

Bircher muesli

✱✱✱ Bircher museli has been around for a long time and is often seen at health farms across Europe. Apparently the original version included cream, but I keep mine fresh and light with Greek yogurt. In this version, I've added sour cherries, but you can adapt the recipe to create your own variations. You do have to start the process the night before, but it involves minimal effort. And even if you don't manage to soak it the night before, it's no biggie – just soak it for 10–15 minutes in the morning.

1073 ENERGY KJ	256 ENERGY KCAL	8.4g PROTEIN	11.7g FAT	1g SATURATED FAT	31.1g CARBOHYDRATES	6.4g TOTAL SUGARS	5.7g FIBRE	0+g SALT

MAKES 30 servings
500g rolled oats
500g spelt flakes
300g flaked almonds
**200g whole hazelnuts, roughly
    chopped**
200g golden raisins
100g sunflower seeds
100g pumpkin seeds
50g dried sour cherries, chopped

To serve (per portion)
100ml apple juice
½ apple, cored and grated
100g thick Greek yogurt

Simply mix all the dry ingredients together and store in an airtight container. The mixture will keep for 4–6 weeks.

When you want to have some for breakfast, make a portion up. This is best done the night before, but preparing it 10–15 minutes before eating will do if you are pushed for time. Simply mix 100g of the dry mixture with the apple juice, grated apple and yogurt. Leave to soak (ideally overnight in the fridge), then serve.

Baked macadamia, pistachio and sour cherry granola

★★☆ *It's taken me a while to develop a baked granola recipe that I am totally happy with, and this is finally it! It is not overly sweet, but it does have a lovely, creamy nuttiness from the coconut oil. I've used some really luxurious ingredients: the Macadamia nuts are big, rich and textured, the pistachios are vibrant and waxy and the sour cherries really add a depth of flavour. Please do experiment: I think the addition of flaxseed would be great, but mix and match according to what you have handy. Hazelnuts and cacao nibs would be good in autumn, while cinnamon and dried apples would work especially well in winter. Just get creative! This is my favourite combo, but you can find your own, too. Bake a big batch of it and have it ready to go for a quick breakfast option.*

1074 ENERGY KJ	257 ENERGY KCAL	7.1g PROTEIN	12.7g FAT	3.6g SATURATED FAT	30.5g CARBOHYDRATES	11.9g TOTAL SUGARS	6.1g FIBRE	0.2g SALT

MAKES 20 servings

150g **runny honey**

2 tablespoons **coconut oil**

½ teaspoon **sea salt flakes**

300g **jumbo rolled oats**

200g **rye flakes**

50g **coconut flakes**

100g **pumpkin seeds**

100g **macadamia nuts, chopped**

100g **Iranian pistachios (standard pistachios will do if you can't get these, but the colour is not as impressive)**

2 **free-range egg whites**

100g **dried sour cherries**

100g **dried apricots, chopped**

Preheat the oven to 140°C/gas mark 1 and line a baking sheet with greaseproof paper.

Melt the honey, coconut oil and sea salt flakes together in a saucepan over a gentle heat.

Place the oats, rye flakes, coconut flakes, pumpkin seeds, macadamia nuts and pistachios in a large bowl and mix together. Add the coconut oil mixture and stir well.

Whisk the egg whites in a separate bowl for about 3 minutes until just combined, then stir into the granola mixture to coat.

Spread the mixture out in an even layer on the prepared baking sheet and bake for about 30 minutes until golden and crispy. Stir and break up occasionally to separate the grains a bit.

Once it's baked, remove from the oven, mix in the dried fruit and leave to cool before transferring to an airtight container to use at will. The granola will keep for 2 weeks.

Goji berry and pistachio granola bars

★★✦ *Shop-bought cereal bars are a big no-no, so if you do opt for them, this is the way to have them. I am not a huge advocate of eating cereal bars for breakfast, as I think a decent protein-based brekkie is better, but a lot of people don't like breakfast or don't have time to make it every morning. So if you are one of them, these bars are for you! You can prepare them over the weekend, or any time you have a spare half hour or so, and then just eat one in the morning. I have added a few little nutritional boosters in the form of Goji berries – they are regarded as one of the planet's superfoods, full of antioxidants while containing less sugar than other dried fruits. I've also used natural sugars here to make these bars healthier. It's still sugar, though, so eat in moderation.*

843 ENERGY KJ	201 ENERGY KCAL	6.4g PROTEIN	6.8g FAT	0.7g SATURATED FAT	30.7g CARBOHYDRATES	16.7g TOTAL SUGARS	5.6g FIBRE	0.2g SALT

MAKES about 15 bars

butter, coconut oil or olive oil,
   for greasing
130g pitted Agen prunes
150g runny honey
2½ tablespoons maple syrup
1 teaspoon vanilla extract
1 teaspoon ground cinnamon
pinch of sea salt
285g rolled oats
100g dried apricots, chopped
100g pistachios
50g sunflower seeds
100g goji berries

Preheat the oven to 160°C/gas mark 3. Lightly grease a 23cm square baking tin with butter, coconut oil or olive oil.

Soak the prunes in hot water for 10 minutes. Drain and place the soaked prunes in a blender along with the honey, maple syrup, vanilla extract, cinnamon and salt. Blitz to make a paste.

Transfer the paste to a large bowl and mix in the oats, apricots, pistachios, sunflower seeds and goji berries. Press the mixture into the prepared tin and bake for 25–30 minutes until it is starting to turn golden brown. Keep an eye on it, as you don't want it to get too brown.

Remove from the oven and leave to cool in the tin, then cut into 15 bars.

These bars will keep for up to 10 days in an airtight container.

Quinoa, papaya and coconut breakfast bar

★★☆ *This is another bar to make ahead that can be grabbed and eaten on the go for those peeps who aren't keen on a cooked breakfast. The quinoa is a great source of protein, while the nuts and coconut oil provide good fats to keep you going.*

1176 ENERGY KJ	284 ENERGY KCAL	2.3g PROTEIN	21.2g FAT	14.1g SATURATED FAT	20.9g CARBOHYDRATES	12.5g TOTAL SUGARS	2.9g FIBRE	0.1g SALT

MAKES about 15 bars

100g pitted dried dates,
    finely chopped

200g coconut oil, plus extra
    for greasing

zest and juice of 1 lime

500g cooked quinoa

50g desiccated coconut

100g macadamia nuts, chopped

50g dried papaya, chopped into
    small to medium pieces

100g dried mango, chopped into
    small to medium pieces

Preheat the oven to 160°C/gas mark 3. Lightly grease a 20 x 15cm baking tin with coconut oil.

Soak the dates in hot water for 10 minutes, then finely chop and add to a saucepan along with the coconut oil and lime zest and juice. Place over a medium heat and warm through.

Place the remaining ingredients in a large bowl and pour over the date and coconut oil mixture. Mix it all together well, then transfer to the prepared tin, spreading the mixture out and pressing it in.

Bake for 20 minutes until golden. Leave to cool in the tin, then cut into bars. The bars will keep for 5–7 days in an airtight container.

Protein hotcakes

✶✶✶ *These pancakes are a bit like a quick, easy version of ricotta hotcakes. Cottage cheese doesn't sound like a very sexy ingredient, but in fact it's great in pancakes like these. If you want to make these into savoury pancakes, simply add some herbs and perhaps serve with bacon rather than agave. I am pretty obsessed with having protein at breakfast, and here we have a good amount of it – in the guise of pancakes, which makes them an appealing choice for children, too. If you're seriously exercising, you could pop in a spoonful of protein powder as well.*

1058 ENERGY KJ	253 ENERGY KCAL	12.4g PROTEIN	3.8g FAT	1.4g SATURATED FAT	48.3g CARBOHYDRATES	6.3g TOTAL SUGARS	7.1g FIBRE	0.9 SALT

SERVES 4

250g wholemeal spelt flour

½ teaspoon baking powder

½ teaspoon ground flaxseed

pinch of salt

½ free-range egg, beaten

110ml buttermilk

1 tablespoon cottage cheese

2 teaspoons oil, for frying (I use
   coconut, but you can use any you
   have handy)

agave syrup and butter, to serve

Mix all the dry ingredients together in one bowl and the egg, buttermilk and cottage cheese together in another bowl. Now pour the wet ingredients into the dry ingredients and mix together.

Heat up a touch of oil in a large frying pan over a medium heat. Spoon a large spoonful of the batter mixture into the frying pan for each hotcake – you should be able to fit more than one in the pan at once. Cook for 3 minutes, then flip over and cook for another 3 minutes on the other side. Transfer the hotcakes to a plate in a low oven to keep them warm while you repeat with the remaining batter and oil.

Serve with butter and agave syrup.

Banana and macadamia nut bread

✳✳✳ *This banana bread is moist and flavoursome. The spelt flour is much easier to digest than wheat flour and it doesn't make your tummy bloat. I used to make banana bread all the time when I was in Australia, and if we didn't eat it all in one sitting, we would slice it and chargrill it the following day to eat with Greek yogurt and blueberries.*

1939 ENERGY KJ	465 ENERGY KCAL	8.7g PROTEIN	25.7g FAT	9g SATURATED FAT	53.9g CARBOHYDRATES	30.8g TOTAL SUGARS	6.8g FIBRE	0.8g SALT

SERVES 6

4 ripe bananas, mashed into a pulp

75g butter, melted, plus extra
    for greasing

100g coconut sugar

50g stevia

1 tablespoon vanilla extract

2 free-range eggs

200g white spelt flour

1 teaspoon bicarbonate of soda

100g macadamia nuts, roughly
    chopped

full-fat Greek yogurt and
    blueberries, to serve (optional)

Preheat the oven to 160°C/gas mark 3. Grease a 900g loaf tin with butter and line with greaseproof paper.

Place the mashed bananas in a large bowl with the melted butter, coconut sugar, stevia, vanilla extract and eggs and mix together well. Add the flour, bicarbonate of soda and macadamia nuts, and stir to combine.

Pour the mixture into the prepared loaf tin and bake for 50–60 minutes until a skewer inserted into the middle comes out clean. Remove from the oven and leave to cool in the tin for 10 minutes, before transferring the loaf to a wire rack to cool completely.

Serve with a dollop of full-fat Greek yogurt, if you like, and some blueberries. If you're eating the loaf a few days after baking, chargrill it to freshen it up and warm it through. It will keep for about 3 days in an airtight container.

SAVOURY

Rye toast four ways

★★★ *Wheat-free rye toast is the only sort of bread I recommend eating in the morning. Sometimes I might have some gluten-free toast, but I find rye keeps me fuller for longer. It's a great choice for a quick breakfast and the best way to eat it is with some proteins. My fall-back rye topping is avocado and chilli sauce, but below are some different ideas. None of this is written in stone – they're just suggestions, so experiment. Think smorgasbord: the list of toppings is endless, although I tend to always try and find a good protein and full flavours. I haven't given any method for these – just pile on and enjoy.*

Smoked mackerel, cucumber pickle, sesame, soy and chilli oil

1163 ENERGY KJ	280 ENERGY KCAL	12.5g PROTEIN	21g FAT	4g SATURATED FAT	12.3g CARBOHYDRATES	1g TOTAL SUGARS	2g FIBRE	2g SALT

PER SLICE

½ smoked mackerel fillet, skinned and any remaining bones removed

1 tablespoon Cucumber Pickle (see page 119)

drizzle of sesame oil, soy sauce and chilli oil

sprinkling of sesame seeds

Peanut butter, chicken and sweet chilli

776 ENERGY KJ	184 ENERGY KCAL	7.3g PROTEIN	5.9g FAT	0.2g SATURATED FAT	26.6g CARBOHYDRATES	3.3g TOTAL SUGARS	1.8g FIBRE	0.4g SALT

PER SLICE

1 tablespoon crunchy peanut butter

100g cooked chicken

drizzle of sweet chilli sauce

Wild mushroom with garlic and herb cream cheese

436 ENERGY KJ	104 ENERGY KCAL	7.3g PROTEIN	5.9g FAT	0.1g SATURATED FAT	26.6g CARBOHYDRATES	3.3g TOTAL SUGARS	1g FIBRE	0.4g SALT

PER SLICE

50g garlic and herb cream cheese, such as Boursin

100g pan-fried wild mushrooms

squeeze of lemon

Avocado and chilli

637 ENERGY KJ	153 ENERGY KCAL	3.2g PROTEIN	10.2g FAT	2.5g SATURATED FAT	13g CARBOHYDRATES	1.3g TOTAL SUGARS	4.5g FIBRE	1.6g SALT

PER SLICE

½ avocado, peeled, stoned and sliced

squeeze of lime juice

pinch of dried chilli flakes or a drizzle of Sriracha chilli sauce

salt and freshly ground black pepper

Tomato and feta baked eggs

★★ *This breakfast is something we make in Greece quite a lot. My parents have lived there for 15 years and it really feels like home now – plus, the food is amazing. When I make this dish, I use up old tomatoes, feta, onions, etc. Sometimes olives get thrown in, sometimes some chilli makes the grade... it really depends what I have at hand. This dish is similar to the Turkish dish Shakshuka, and variations can be found all over Southern Europe and the Middle East.*

1503 ENERGY KJ	361 ENERGY KCAL	21.9g PROTEIN	26.2g FAT	10.5g SATURATED FAT	10.4g CARBOHYDRATES	8.1g TOTAL SUGARS	2.5g FIBRE	3.6g SALT

SERVES 2

splash of olive oil

1 garlic clove, chopped

1 onion, chopped

1 x 400g can tomatoes

4 free-range eggs

1 teaspoon dried oregano

100g feta cheese

salt and freshly ground black pepper

fresh oregano leaves, to garnish
   (optional)

Heat the oil in a large frying pan with a heatproof handle. Add the garlic and onion and fry for 8–10 minutes until translucent.

Add the tomatoes, season with salt and pepper and cook for about 15 minutes.

Preheat the grill to high.

Make four little indentations in the tomatoes and crack the eggs into these spaces. Continue to cook for 3 minutes on the hob, then sprinkle over the oregano and feta and pop the pan under the grill for a few minutes until the eggs are cooked to your liking. Serve, scattered with fresh oregano leaves (if using).

Baked Portobello mushrooms with spinach and garlic cream cheese

★★✫ *This recipe is a great way to include more veggies at breakfast time, and it's also good to have something different that vegetarians can enjoy – it is harder to go on a protein-based diet if you're veggie. This dish is quick, simple and tasty, as well as easy to adapt. You can swap the cream cheese for goat's cheese or Camembert... whatever you prefer.*

| 714 ENERGY KJ | 171 ENERGY KCAL | 13g PROTEIN | 11.1g FAT | 2.7g SATURATED FAT | 4.7g CARBOHYDRATES | 4.3g TOTAL SUGARS | 4.6g FIBRE | 1g SALT |

SERVES 4

8 large Portobello mushrooms,
    peeled and stalks removed
1 teaspoon olive oil
300g spinach leaves
200g garlic and herb cream cheese,
    such as Boursin
50g Parmesan cheese, grated
salt and freshly ground black pepper

Preheat the grill to high.

Place the mushrooms on a baking tray, drizzle with the oil and season with salt and pepper. Place under the grill and cook for 3 minutes on each side.

Whilst the mushrooms are cooking, rinse the spinach in cold water, then place in a saucepan and wilt over a gentle heat. Drain off any remaining water.

Turn the mushrooms stalk-side up and place a little spinach in each one. Top with some of the cream cheese and Parmesan. Place back under the grill until golden.

Creamy goat's cheese and herb omelette with dressed salad leaves

★★☆ *This is a very simple but quite refined omelette; it is classically French. The creamy, peppery cheese melts through the middle, complemented by the touch of herbs and dressed greens. Don't think that serving salad with breakfast is strange either – it's a good way to get in more veggies and it really balances the dish. Being a chef is all about balancing flavours, and this dish exemplifies the need for that finesse.*

1046 ENERGY KJ	252 ENERGY KCAL	15.8g PROTEIN	20.6g FAT	7g SATURATED FAT	1.5g CARBOHYDRATES	1.3g TOTAL SUGARS	1.7g FIBRE	2.6g SALT

SERVES 1

2 free-range eggs

a handful of freshly chopped chives

½ teaspoon olive oil

1 tablespoon soft goat's cheese

a handful of mixed salad leaves

1 teaspoon lemon juice

1 teaspoon olive oil

sea salt and freshly ground
    black pepper

Preheat the grill to high.

In a bowl, whisk the eggs up with a little salt and pepper and the chives. Then heat the oil in a little omelette pan or small frying pan with a heatproof handle and pour in the egg and chive mixture. Let it settle for a minute, then use a spatula to pull the sides away from the edges and ruffle the mixture up a bit. Sprinkle the cheese in a line down the middle of the eggs.

Now pop the pan under the grill for about a minute – you don't want to overcook the omelette.

Once it's cooked, fold the omelette over and transfer to a plate. Dress the salad leaves by drizzling over the lemon juice and olive oil, and serve.

Huevos rancheros

✖✖✖ *This is my ideal brunch: you have chilli, tomatoes, protein, good carbs and great fats with the avocado. You want colour and brightness in the morning, and this gives you all of that. In LA you can find this hybrid Mexican food everywhere, and you get so much choice at breakfast time, which I think is really positive. The food scene in California is a HUGE inspiration to me and I love the vibrant way they put food together. The English breakfast is well known, of course, but variety is good for you and I don't think we have enough of that in the UK. To reduce the carbs, leave out the tortillas.*

2483 ENERGY KJ	591 ENERGY KCAL	29.8g PROTEIN	25.4g FAT	9.1g SATURATED FAT	65.6g CARBOHYDRATES	11g TOTAL SUGARS	19.8g FIBRE	0.5g SALT

SERVES 2

1 teaspoon olive oil, plus extra for the eggs

1 onion, diced

½ teaspoon ground cumin

pinch of dried chilli flakes

1 x 400g can black beans, drained and rinsed

4 corn tortillas

2 free-range eggs

75g feta cheese, crumbled

salt and freshly ground black pepper

For the guacamole

1 avocado, peeled and stoned

a small handful of freshly chopped coriander, plus extra to serve

juice of 1 lime

½ garlic clove, peeled

For the salsa

4 ripe tomatoes, diced

½ red onion, diced

a small handful of freshly chopped coriander

dash of Tabasco sauce

Heat the oil in a small saucepan over a medium heat. Add the onion, cumin and chilli flakes and fry until the onion is translucent. Add the beans and 100ml water, season with salt and pepper and simmer for about 10 minutes.

For the guacamole, place all the ingredients in a blender and blitz until smooth. Season with salt and pepper, then set aside.

For the salsa, mix all the ingredients together in a bowl. Season with salt and pepper, then set aside.

When you are ready to eat, fry the tortillas in a hot, dry frying pan for a few minutes on each side until golden and browned, transferring them to a low grill or oven to keep warm.

In a separate pan, fry the eggs to your liking in a touch of olive oil. When the eggs are ready, get out two plates. On each plate, place two tortillas, then some beans on top. Make a well in the middle of the beans and place a fried egg in the well.

Sprinkle with the feta and some coriander leaves, and serve with a large dollop of the guacamole and the salsa.

Big Sur eggs benedict

★★☆ *I am a huge fan of Californian food and cooking. I went to Big Sur recently and I was bowled over by how stunning it is. At the hotel I stayed at, they served Eggs Benedict with a layer of avocado underneath the egg and called it 'California Eggs Benedict'. To make it fit in with my low-carb eating plan, I swapped the muffin for some chicken sausages, and that's how my Big Sur Eggs Benedict came about. It's now one of my favourite brunch dishes.*

1320 ENERGY KJ	317 ENERGY KCAL	36g PROTEIN	18.2g FAT	4.2g SATURATED FAT	2.3g CARBOHYDRATES	1.5g TOTAL SUGARS	3.9g FIBRE	1.8g SALT

SERVES 4

2 avocados, peeled and stoned

juice of 1 lime

a small handful of freshly chopped
　　coriander

4 free-range eggs

2 teaspoons olive oil

200g spinach leaves

sea salt and freshly ground
　　black pepper

Hollandaise sauce, to serve (see
　　page 119)

For the turkey patties

500g turkey mince

4 spring onions, finely sliced

1 red chilli, diced

First, make the patties. In a large bowl, mix together all the ingredients and some seasoning. Once the mixture is combined, use your hand to shape it into four patties, each measuring about 10cm wide and 2.5cm deep. Place the patties on a plate in the fridge to chill and firm up.

In a bowl, mash the avocados together with the lime juice and coriander, and season with salt and pepper.

Place a large, non-stick frying pan over a high heat. When the pan is hot, add the patties and dry-fry for 6 minutes on each side or until cooked through. Once cooked, transfer the patties to a plate in a low oven to keep them warm while you prepare the rest of the dish.

Poach the eggs according to the method on page 50. While they are poaching, heat the oil in a saucepan over a high heat and add the spinach for a few minutes to wilt. Stir in some salt and pepper.

When everything is ready, you can assemble. Take out four plates and place a patty on each one. Top each patty with a layer of spinach, some crushed avocado, an egg and finally a touch of Hollandaise Sauce. I often serve this with some baby salad leaves and cherry tomatoes on the side.

Green eggs

★☆☆ *When I am seriously trying to lose weight or am in my first 2 weeks of eating more healthily, then this breakfast, or variations of it, is what I tend to have. A good load of green veggies for breakfast sets me up really well and gives me energy. If I need some carbs, I simply stir through some cooked quinoa. This recipe is a great way to use up leftover veggies, and I actually cook too many on purpose now for this reason.*

765 ENERGY KJ	184 ENERGY KCAL	14.2g PROTEIN	13.2g FAT	3.1g SATURATED FAT	2.3g CARBOHYDRATES	1.8g TOTAL SUGARS	2.4g FIBRE	1.7g SALT

SERVES 4

8 free-range eggs

1 teaspoon olive oil

1 onion, sliced

1 courgette, diced

100g cooked broccoli

150g cooked spinach leaves, chopped

salt and freshly ground black pepper

For the pesto

1 garlic clove

3 large handfuls of basil

1 tablespoon pine nuts, lightly roasted

30g Parmesan cheese, grated

100ml extra virgin olive oil

Begin by making the pesto. Simply place all the pesto ingredients in a blender and pulse to combine. Don't blitz them too much – it's better to keep a bit of texture. You can add a splash of water to loosen the mixture up if needed. Set aside.

Crack the eggs into a bowl and whisk together.

Heat the olive oil in a frying pan over a medium heat. Add the onion and courgette and cook for about 8 minutes, then season. Now add the broccoli and spinach, heat through and season again.

Finally, add the eggs with 1 tablespoon of the pesto and cook until the eggs reach your desired consistency. I cook these for quite a while, but it's down to personal preference – although you should cook them for at least 4 minutes.

Chef's tip: *If I feel like I need some carbs, I serve these eggs with 2 tablespoons cooked quinoa per person stirred in.*

Coconut oil and brown rice kedgeree

✷✷✷ *Rice for breakfast may seem strange to Western tastes, but in fact it makes a fantastic choice to start your day. Brown rice is a great complex carb, so it keeps you full for longer. The coconut oil adds a gorgeous flavour, and smoked salmon provides protein. Traditional kedgeree uses smoked haddock, but with the hot smoked salmon you cut out that cooking process, making it a much quicker recipe. Serve this kedgeree topped with a soft-yolk poached egg, so that when you break into it the yolk drizzles down over the rice.*

1485 ENERGY KJ	354 ENERGY KCAL	22.8g PROTEIN	15g FAT	7.1g SATURATED FAT	34.4g CARBOHYDRATES	1.7g TOTAL SUGARS	1.8g FIBRE	3g SALT

SERVES 2

1 tablespoon coconut oil, plus extra if frying the eggs

6 spring onions, sliced

2 garlic cloves, finely chopped

1 red chilli, finely chopped

1 teaspoon garam masala

½ teaspoon ground turmeric

200g cooked brown rice

100g hot smoked salmon

1 teaspoon Bragg's Liquid Aminos (I use this instead of soy sauce for its added health qualities, but wheat-free tamari is good, too)

1 tablespoon freshly chopped coriander

2 tablespoons white wine vinegar

2 free-range eggs

sriracha chilli sauce and lime wedges, to serve

Start by heating the coconut oil in a large frying pan over a medium heat. Add the spring onions, along with the garlic and chilli, and fry until the onions are translucent. Now add the spices and fry for a further minute.

Add the cooked rice and smoked salmon to the pan and cook for about 5 minutes before adding the Aminos or tamari. Finally, check the seasoning and add the coriander.

Meanwhile, poach the eggs. Simply add the vinegar to a saucepan of water and place over a high heat to boil. When the water is lightly bubbling, crack the eggs into the water one at a time and cook for 3–5 minutes depending on how you like them done. Once cooked, scoop the eggs out with a slotted spoon. If you prefer, you can fry the eggs – either fry in a separate frying pan with a little coconut oil or, once the rice mixture is ready, transfer it to a covered bowl and fry the eggs in the now empty pan.

To serve, place a pile of rice on each plate and top with an egg. Serve with some lime wedges and sriracha chilli sauce on the side.

Chef's tip: *I like to poach my eggs when the bubbles in the water are very light and delicate. It is easier to crack the eggs into this calmer water, and the bubbles gently lift the egg up.*

Truffle and Parmesan scrambled eggs with Parma ham

✴︎✴︎✴︎ This breakfast just feels luxurious. I had this first when I was in Venice one winter for a weekend and it has stuck in my mind. My memory is made up of my food experiences around the globe – if you ask me what I was doing last week, I would have to check my diary to remember, but this breakfast, 5 years ago in the Danieli Hotel, is crystal clear. The Parma ham and Parmesan give masses of flavour, and I couldn't resist a drizzle of truffle oil. This is a great example of how a simple dish like scrambled eggs can be perked up really easily.

1281 ENERGY KJ	308 ENERGY KCAL	27.2g PROTEIN	23g FAT	9.6g SATURATED FAT	0.3g CARBOHYDRATES	0.3g TOTAL SUGARS	0g FIBRE	2.6g SALT

SERVES 4

8 free-range eggs

splash of semi-skimmed milk

tiny knob of butter

100g aged Parmesan cheese, shaved

drizzle of truffle oil

8 slices Parma Ham

salt and freshly ground black pepper

Whisk together the eggs and milk in a bowl and season with salt and pepper. Place a non-stick saucepan over a medium heat and add the butter. Once it has melted, pour in the egg mixture. Stir well and cook until thick and creamy.

Divide between four plates and serve with a good covering of Parmesan shavings, a drizzle of truffle oil and two slices of Parma ham per plate.

Avocado, chicken and jalapeño frittata

★★ *Frittatas are your friend when following a low-carb diet. If you're short on time in the mornings, you can make them the night before and have a cold wedge for breakfast. They're amazingly versatile, too, as you can change the fillings to suit your preference or what you have to hand – smoked fish, bacon, cheese and veggies all work really well. I like this recipe because of the double protein whammy of the chicken and eggs, the creamy fat of the avocado and the tiny chilli spike of the jalapeños.*

1743 ENERGY KJ	418 ENERGY KCAL	43.6g PROTEIN	26.6g FAT	10.1g SATURATED FAT	1.1g CARBOHYDRATES	0.7g TOTAL SUGARS	1.7g FIBRE	2.2g SALT

SERVES 4

10 free-range eggs

300g cooked chicken breast,
    shredded

1 avocado, peeled, stoned and sliced

100g drained pickled jalapeños

100g mature Cheddar cheese, grated

sea salt and freshly ground
    black pepper

Preheat the grill to high.

Crack the eggs into a bowl and whisk with some salt and pepper. Heat a medium-sized frying pan with a heatproof handle over a medium heat. Add the chicken and stir to warm through. Now add the avocado, then pour in the egg mixture.

Let the mixture settle around the edges of the pan, then pull in the sides with a spatula. Make sure the chicken and avocado are spread out evenly, then sprinkle over the jalapeños and the cheese.

Cook for a few more minutes on the hob, before placing the pan underneath the grill. Cook for a few minutes more until just set and then serve.

Heirloom tomatoes, basil and aioli on toast

★☆☆ *Heirloom vegetables are very popular now, but all 'heirloom' really means is different or older varieties of vegetable. Supermarkets have caused us to become accustomed to fresh produce being very standardised – we only expect to see one shape, one size and one type of tomato, carrot or cauliflower. This isn't realistic – vegetables don't all grow the same way. This recipe is a simple but gorgeous way to use the summer glut of tomatoes in all their shapes, colours and sizes. Tomatoes are the staple of many of my meals, partly because they contain the great antioxidant lycopene, but also in that they add a savoury umami flavour to food that I can't get enough of.*

1552 ENERGY KJ	374 ENERGY KCAL	5.6g PROTEIN	30.8g FAT	5g SATURATED FAT	19.8g CARBOHYDRATES	3.4g TOTAL SUGARS	2.2g FIBRE	1.9g SALT

SERVES 4
300g heirloom tomatoes
splash of Classic Dressing (page 68)
4 slices spelt bread
a small handful of basil leaves
salt and freshly ground black pepper

For the aioli
2 pasteurised free-range egg yolks
2 garlic cloves, finely crushed
100ml extra virgin olive oil
1 teaspoon lemon juice

Begin by making the aioli. Place the egg yolks and garlic in a blender, then, with the blender running, gradually add the oil until the mixture thickens and becomes pale. Do not add the oil too quickly, as the mixture will split. Season with salt and pepper and add the lemon juice.

Slice the tomatoes into different shapes and sizes and add to a bowl. Season and add the dressing, then mix well.

Toast the spelt bread, then spread each slice with the aioli. Top with the tomatoes and basil and serve.

Smoked paprika, chorizo and pancetta baked beans

★★☆ *This simple recipe is a meal in itself. It's a take on American baked beans, with smoked pancetta and a touch of maple syrup. Serve it with a fried or poached egg on top for a filling breakfast. This dish is great for the diet, as it means that you get really good proteins and carbs in the morning and you can also make it ahead of time.*

1309 ENERGY KJ	313 ENERGY KCAL	18.7g PROTEIN	15.4g FAT	5.2g SATURATED FAT	26.5g CARBOHYDRATES	15.6g TOTAL SUGARS	7.9g FIBRE	3.6g SALT

SERVES 4

1 tablespoon olive oil

1 onion, diced

100g chorizo sausage, chopped

150g smoked pancetta, chopped

1 teaspoon smoked paprika

1 x 400g can haricot beans, drained
    and rinsed

300ml tomato passata

1 teaspoon balsamic vinegar

1 tablespoon maple syrup

sea salt and freshly ground
    black pepper

Preheat the oven to 180°C/gas mark 4.

Heat the olive oil in a heavy-bottomed casserole dish over a medium heat. Add the onion, chorizo and pancetta to the pan and fry for 8–10 minutes until the lovely oils and flavours have come out of the meat.

Add the smoked paprika, beans, passata, balsamic vinegar and maple syrup and stir well, then season to taste. Bring to the boil and then place the casserole dish in the oven, uncovered, for 30 minutes before serving.

This is great served with a fried or poached egg on top.

Smoked salmon plate with homemade pickles, beetroot horseradish and rye

★★☆ *When I am craving New York, this is the dish I make. It has all those components of my fave New York deli meals of beetroot, horseradish, smoked salmon and crunchy rye breadcrumbs, plus it includes a fab quick pickle recipe. Wheat-free rye bread is great to have around for a quick breakfast, and this uses some for the crunch factor. As well as bringing back fond memories of my travels, this dish is high in nutritional benefits, too: great fats and proteins, some complex carbs with the beetroot and rye and some antioxidants to round it off.*

1814 ENERGY KJ	434 ENERGY KCAL	32.8g PROTEIN	21g FAT	11.1g SATURATED FAT	28.6g CARBOHYDRATES	6.1g TOTAL SUGARS	5.1g FIBRE	1.3g SALT

SERVES 4

200g stale rye bread

400g smoked salmon

150ml crème fraîche

lemon wedges, to serve (optional)

For the beetroot horseradish

2 medium raw beetroots

10cm piece of fresh horseradish

50ml white wine vinegar

For the quick dill pickles

2 tablespoons stevia

200ml white wine vinegar

a small handful of freshly
    chopped dill

1 teaspoon mustard seeds

4 small Lebanese cucumbers (baby
    cucumbers will do if you can't
    get Lebanese)

1 teaspoon salt

Start by making the beetroot horseradish. Peel and then finely grate the beetroot and the horseradish into a bowl. Stir in the vinegar, then set aside for 10 minutes.

To make the rye crumbs, preheat the oven to 150°C/gas mark 2. Crumble up the bread using your fingers and spread out on a baking tray. Place in the oven for about 30 minutes until the crumbs are completely dried out. If you're not going to use them right away, leave them to cool, then transfer to an airtight container.

To make the pickles, place the stevia, vinegar, dill and mustard seeds in a pan. Simmer for 5 minutes, then take off the heat and leave to cool.

Finely slice the cucumbers and rub the slices with the salt. Leave to sit for 5 minutes, then wash off the salt and add the cucumber to the vinegar mixture.

Arrange the smoked salmon on a platter, and serve with the beetroot horseradish, cucumber pickle and the crème fraîche. Finally, sprinkle over the rye crumbs for texture. If you like, you could also serve with some lemon wedges.

Buckwheat blinis with smoked salmon, vodka-spiked sour cream and salmon keta

★★☆ *Buckwheat flour is a great wheat-free flour and is classically used for blinis. It adds more flavour to the pancakes and tastes perfect with smoked salmon. I have added a touch of vodka to the sour cream – it delivers a sourness and spike that I love when paired with this dish. I finish this plate with jewel-like keta (salmon roe/eggs). They are like little pods of Omega-3 goodness and they look stunning.*

2069 ENERGY KJ	496 ENERGY KCAL	29g PROTEIN	26.3g FAT	12.8g SATURATED FAT	37g CARBOHYDRATES	4.5g TOTAL SUGARS	1.1g FIBRE	1.9g SALT

SERVES 4

300g smoked salmon

1 tablespoon keta (salmon roe)

salt and freshly ground black pepper

For the sour cream

150ml sour cream

½ teaspoon lemon zest

splash of vodka

For the blinis

200g buckwheat flour

2 teaspoons baking powder

300ml semi-skimmed milk

2 free-range eggs

½ teaspoon olive oil, for frying

For the sour cream mixture, simply place the sour cream, lemon zest and vodka in a bowl. Mix together, season and set aside.

For the blini mix, place the buckwheat flour and baking powder in a bowl with some salt and pepper. In a separate bowl or jug, whisk the milk and eggs together. Gradually whisk the liquids into the dry ingredients until a smooth batter is achieved.

Place a non-stick frying pan or blini pan (see tip below) over a medium heat and add a splash of oil. Spoon about 2 tablespoons of the batter into the pan for each pancake – you might be able to cook more than one at a time, depending on the size of your pan. Cook for about 4 minutes until golden brown, then flip over and cook for another 4 minutes on the other side. When cooked through, transfer to a plate in a low oven to keep warm and repeat the process with the rest of the batter.

When all the blinis are ready, top each one with the smoked salmon, keta and some sour cream mixture, and serve.

Chef's tip: *You can get blini pans, which are small frying pans. They are a great investment for all your pancake needs.*

Lighter Meals

Pea and truffle soup

★☆☆ This soup is quick to make but is restaurant standard. The key is not to cook the peas too much; this retains their bright green hues and fresh flavour. I decorate this dish with truffled-up goat's curd and borage flowers. I don't use edible flowers just because they are in fashion – my grandfather used to decorate his homemade soup with them when I was little, and one of my favourite cookbooks when I was growing up was about cooking with flowers and herbs. They add a bit of magic.

1215 ENERGY KJ	292 ENERGY KCAL	14.7g PROTEIN	19.9g FAT	12.4g SATURATED FAT	14.8g CARBOHYDRATES	5.3g TOTAL SUGARS	7.3g FIBRE	1.6g SALT

SERVES 8

100g butter

4 shallots, chopped

750ml vegetable stock

2 x 500g bags frozen peas

250g fresh goat's curd

1 tablespoon chopped canned
    truffles

½ teaspoon white truffle oil (**Urbani
    is a good brand**)

**sea salt and freshly ground
    black pepper**

borage flowers, to garnish

Heat the butter in a large saucepan over a low heat. Once it's melted, add the shallots and gently fry for 5–10 minutes, being careful not to let them colour.

Add the stock and bring to the boil. Then add the peas and bring to the boil again.

Take off the heat and drain the peas, reserving the liquid. Blitz the cooked peas in a blender until smooth. With the blender still running, gradually pour in the reserved liquid until you reach the desired consistency. Season to taste.

Return the soup to the pan to warm through. Meanwhile, mix the goat's curd, truffles and truffle oil together in a small bowl.

To serve, ladle the soup into bowls and add a few dollops of the goat's curd mixture to each. Scatter over the flowers and serve.

Tomato and crème fraîche soup

★✩✩ *This is my souped-up version of the classic canned tomato soup we all grew up with in the UK. A bowl of this with some chunks of Cheddar cheese melting inside really does make you happy – plus it's quick to make when you are in a rush. The antioxidant lycopene is concentrated when the tomatoes are cooked, so you are getting a health boost, too.*

733 ENERGY KJ	177 ENERGY KCAL	2.2g PROTEIN	16.5g FAT	7.7g SATURATED FAT	5.4g CARBOHYDRATES	4.3g TOTAL SUGARS	1.3g FIBRE	0.9g SALT

SERVES 8

50ml olive oil, plus extra for drizzling

2 garlic cloves, chopped

2 banana shallots, finely diced

a pinch of dried chilli flakes

1 x 400g can chopped tomatoes

400ml vegetable stock

1 teaspoon stevia

1 teaspoon salt

2 sprigs of basil, chopped

200g crème fraîche

Heat up the olive oil in a saucepan over a low heat. Add the garlic, shallots and chilli flakes and gently fry until the shallots are translucent.

Add the tomatoes and stock. Bring to the boil and add the stevia and salt, then simmer for 20 minutes. Add the basil and crème fraîche and blitz with a hand blender.

Serve with another drizzle of olive oil and chow down.

Butternut squash and cockle chowder

✳✳✳ *This is a lower-carb version of the classic clam chowder. I've replaced the potatoes with squash because I think the sweetness works well. I've also used British cockles instead of the usual clams, but the latter are fine, too – or you could use smoked haddock.*

2407 ENERGY KJ	574 ENERGY KCAL	39.9g PROTEIN	28.2g FAT	14.9g SATURATED FAT	30.3g CARBOHYDRATES	8.5g TOTAL SUGARS	4.1g FIBRE	0.6g SALT

SERVES 8

For the cockle broth

1.5 litres fish stock

500ml white wine

2 bay leaves

1–2 tablespoons black peppercorns

2kg live Dorset cockles, scrubbed

For the chowder base

1 teaspoon olive oil

4 slices smoked streaky bacon, finely chopped

200g butter

2 celery sticks, finely chopped

1 onion, finely diced

4 garlic cloves, finely chopped

6 spring onions, finely sliced

400g butternut squash, peeled, deseeded and cut into cubes

1kg frozen sweetcorn kernels

a sprig of thyme

salt and freshly ground black pepper

To serve

freshly chopped flat-leaf parsley

squeeze of lemon juice

400ml double cream

Begin by opening the cockles. Place the fish stock, white wine, bay leaves and peppercorns in a large saucepan. Bring to the boil and then add the cockles. Bring back up to the boil and wait for the cockle shells to open. Once they do, take the pan off the heat and use a slotted spoon to fish out all of the cockles, discarding any that refuse to open. Shell three-quarters of the opened cockles (leave the rest with their shells on for presentation) and set aside. Reserve the cooking liquid.

Place another heavy-bottomed saucepan over a medium heat and add a touch of oil, then the bacon. Fry for a few minutes to release the flavour and fat, then add the butter, celery, onion, garlic and spring onions. Continue to sweat to get all the flavours mingling – this should take about 10 minutes.

Add the squash, sweetcorn and thyme, and the reserved liquid from cooking the cockles. Bring to the boil and then simmer for about 30 minutes, until the squash has completely softened.

Season, add all the cockles and cook for 1 minute more. Stir through the chopped parsley, add a squeeze of lemon juice, and serve with the double cream.

Persian-inspired chicken bone broth

★★ *Bone broth is big news right now. Technically, it is just stock cooked for a long time, but who's splitting hairs? You cannot beat a good chicken broth. I am a pedant when it comes to how it is cooked, though. I like to use raw bones, as I think the flavour is better. They say that there is an enzyme that comes out during the cooking process that helps ward off bugs (hence the old theory about chicken soup being the Jewish penicillin). I've added turmeric and spices, to give it an extra heart-warming boost.*

416 ENERGY KJ	99 ENERGY KCAL	10g PROTEIN	4.5g FAT	0.3g SATURATED FAT	6.8g CARBOHYDRATES	4.8g TOTAL SUGARS	2.1g FIBRE	0.7g SALT

SERVES 8

4 raw chicken carcasses

4 carrots, top and tailed but
    left whole

2 leeks, roughly chopped

2 onions, roughly chopped

1 celery stick, roughly chopped

4 garlic cloves, squashed

2–3 bay leaves

1 teaspoon ground turmeric

1 teaspoon ground cumin

2 green chillies, halved

2 limes, halved

To serve

a bunch of fresh flat-leaf parsley,
    chopped

a bunch of fresh mint, chopped

a bunch of fresh coriander, chopped

a bunch of spring onions, chopped

olive oil, to drizzle

Take your largest saucepan and place all the soup ingredients (except the 'to serve' ingredients) in it, along with 6 litres of water.

Bring to the boil, skimming off all the fat and sediment/foam, and then reduce the heat. Keep on a gentle simmer for about 5 hours, topping up with water when required to keep the bones covered.

By the end of the cooking time, the bones and veggies should be soft and falling apart. Drain through a sieve, retaining the stock. Press the mixture in the sieve to get all the flavour out.

Return the stock to the saucepan and add the herbs and spring onions. Season and simmer for another 10 minutes, then serve with a drizzle of olive oil.

Summer chopped salad

✱✱✱ Chopped salads are a great way to get loads of veggies and protein into your diet. I change my chopped salad according to the seasons: this is my summer version, and my winter version is below. Feel free to experiment and put together a salad made up of all your fave items – the key is simply to cut everything the same size. The dressing makes enough for 8–10 salads, and is a great one to have on stand-by, as it goes with just about everything.

1405 ENERGY KJ	337 ENERGY KCAL	31g PROTEIN	19.7g FAT	4.6g SATURATED FAT	8.9g CARBOHYDRATES	5.3g TOTAL SUGARS	4.7g FIBRE	0.4g SALT

per 20g serving of Classic Dressing

460 ENERGY KJ	112 ENERGY KCAL	0.1g PROTEIN	11.7g FAT	1.7g SATURATED FAT	0.3g CARBOHYDRATES	0.3g TOTAL SUGARS	0g FIBRE	0.1g SALT

SERVES 1

a handful of peas

½ little gem lettuce, torn

a handful of diced cooked
    chicken breast

2 cooked asparagus spears, sliced
    and tips set aside

4 cherry tomatoes, halved

2 radishes, thinly sliced

¼ avocado, peeled and diced

1 teaspoon chopped chives

1 teaspoon grated Parmesan cheese

a handful of diced cooked beetroot

For the classic dressing

250ml good-quality Chardonnay
    white wine vinegar

375ml extra virgin olive oil

1 tablespoon Dijon mustard

1 teaspoon runny honey

sea salt and freshly ground
    black pepper

Whisk all the dressing ingredients together in a small bowl. In another bowl, mix all the salad ingredients together, except for the asparagus tips and beetroot. Toss with dressing to taste and season. Transfer to a serving bowl or plate, sprinkle over the beetroot and top with the asparagus tips.

Winter chopped salad

For a winter version, prepare **a handful of little gem lettuce, chiffonade** (see Tip), **a small handful of radicchio, chiffonade, 4 cherry tomatoes, quartered, ½ avocado, peeled, stoned and diced, a handful of diced roasted butternut squash, a small handful of diced Cashel Blue cheese, a small handful of finely sliced fennel, a small handful of diced cooked beetroot** and **a small handful of candied pecans**. Dress with **Classic Dressing** (see left) and season with **sea salt and freshly ground black pepper**.

1908 ENERGY KJ	461 ENERGY KCAL	9.7g PROTEIN	42.8g FAT	8.5g SATURATED FAT
9.6g CARBOHYDRATES	7.2g TOTAL SUGARS	5.8g FIBRE	1.8g SALT	

Chef's tip: *Chiffonade is a chopping technique where ingredients are very finely sliced into long, thin strips.*

Caesar salad

★ ★ ✷ *Caesar salad is found everywhere, but it can vary massively in quality. When made well, it is actually a very beautiful dish and the dressing is quite complex. My secret ingredient is the smoked anchovies, as they lend a beautiful smoked essence to the dish. I also lightly grill the little gem to add depth to the flavour. If you want a bit more crunch (as this version doesn't include the traditional croutons), use my crisp chicken skin recipe (see page 177) and break some over the finished dish.*

758 ENERGY KJ	183 ENERGY KCAL	8.9g PROTEIN	16.1g FAT	3.8g SATURATED FAT	0.7g CARBOHYDRATES	0.6g TOTAL SUGARS	0.3g FIBRE	1.4g SALT

per 20g serving of Caesar Dressing

470 ENERGY KJ	114 ENERGY KCAL	2.2g PROTEIN	11.6g FAT	2.3g SATURATED FAT	0.1g CARBOHYDRATES	0.1g TOTAL SUGARS	0g FIBRE	0.3g SALT

SERVES 4

4 little gem lettuces

1 tablespoon Parmesan
    cheese shavings

4 smoked anchovies

4 soft-boiled quail eggs

For the Caesar dressing

4 anchovy fillets, finely chopped

4 smoked anchovies, finely chopped

2 garlic cloves, finely crushed

200g Parmesan cheese, grated

2 tablespoons Dijon mustard

4 free-range egg yolks

100ml white wine vinegar

500ml light olive oil

juice of 1 lemon

salt and freshly ground black pepper

To make the dressing, place all the anchovies, garlic, cheese, mustard and egg yolks in a food processor and blitz until smooth. Add the vinegar and blitz again. Then, with the blender still running, slowly add the oil, very gradually, until the dressing thickens, rather like mayonnaise. Stir in the lemon juice and season.

To prep the salad leaves, trim the base of each lettuce and discard the outer leaves. Then place a griddle pan over a high heat and chargrill on the flat side for about 4 minutes to get a bit of colour. Set aside to cool.

When you are ready to eat, cut the little gem halves in half and toss in a serving bowl with some dressing – about 1½ tablespoons per person. Top with the Parmesan, anchovies and the eggs.

St Tropez-inspired crudités

★☆☆ My favourite place in the whole world to have lunch is Le Club 55 in St Tropez. It is completely iconic and has been the playground of the rich and famous since the 50s. They serve amazing bowls of crudités, including big, whole, juicy tomatoes, spring onions and artichokes, with an infamous peppery dip. This is my mini version.

331 ENERGY KJ	79 ENERGY KCAL	7.6g PROTEIN	2.1g FAT	0.7g SATURATED FAT	8.2g CARBOHYDRATES	7.6g TOTAL SUGARS	7.0g FIBRE	0.1g SALT

per 48g serving of dip

1129 ENERGY KJ	274 ENERGY KCAL	2.5g PROTEIN	29g FAT	4.5g SATURATED FAT	0.5g CARBOHYDRATES	0.2g TOTAL SUGARS	0.1g FIBRE	0.4g SALT

SERVES 8

For the crudités

use a selection of whatever is in season. I like the following:

6 red and yellow chicory leaves, trimmed

½ large fennel bulb, finely sliced

3 baby heirloom carrots

3 asparagus spears

3 radishes (preferably with leaves)

8–10 cherry vine tomatoes

4–6 cauliflower florets

2 soft-boiled quail eggs

2 cooked baby artichokes

For the dip

2 garlic cloves, crushed

1 tablespoon Dijon mustard

½ tablespoon finely chopped anchovies

40ml white wine vinegar

5 free-range egg yolks

150ml olive oil

50ml vegetable oil

juice of ½ lemon

salt and freshly ground black pepper

Prepare your chosen crudités.

To make the dip, whisk together the garlic, mustard, anchovies, vinegar and egg yolks in a bowl, then slowly pour the oils in, whisking constantly. Season with lots of freshly ground black pepper and sea salt to taste. Stir in the lemon juice.

Serve with the crudités and a glass of Provençal rosé!

The dip will keep for about 1 week in the fridge.

Roast beef, red onion, roasted squash and blue cheese radicchio wraps

*** *I make these to use up my Sunday roast leftovers. I like roasting red onions and squash on a Sunday, and then the day after I make these babies for my lunch. Easy and tasty.*

| 1508 ENERGY KJ | 359 ENERGY KCAL | 40.6g PROTEIN | 15.7g FAT | 8.7g SATURATED FAT | 15.2g CARBOHYDRATES | 9.9g TOTAL SUGARS | 3.7g FIBRE | 0.7g SALT |

SERVES 4

4 large radicchio leaves

4 slices cold roast beef, cut into strips

200g roasted squash

200g roasted onions

100g blue cheese (I like Cashel Blue or Saint Agur)

This is super simple! Just take each radicchio leaf, and layer up the beef, squash, onions and blue cheese. Then roll up and pop in your packed lunch.

Chicken, hummus, sriracha and avocado wraps

*** *I do miss wraps when I am cutting out wheat, but using lettuce leaves is a great alternative. These are really satisfying. I am addicted to hummus, chilli and avocados, so they always get thrown in, but you can experiment and add whatever you want – within reason!*

| 813 ENERGY KJ | 195 ENERGY KCAL | 17.9g PROTEIN | 11.9g FAT | 3.7g SATURATED FAT | 4.1g CARBOHYDRATES | 1.5g TOTAL SUGARS | 1.6g FIBRE | 1.1g SALT |

SERVES 4

4 large iceberg lettuce leaves

100g shop-bought hummus

200g cooked chicken, shredded

50g feta cheese, crumbled

½ avocado, peeled, stoned and sliced

½ cucumber, cut into batons

drizzle of sriracha chilli sauce

Lay out your lettuce leaves and spread the hummus onto each one. Sprinkle over the chicken, feta and avocado.

Finally, lay the cucumber on top and drizzle with the sriracha before rolling up and eating.

Lamb koftas with Beirut chopped salad and tahini yogurt dip

★★⋆ *I lived in Beirut for a year doing restaurant consultancy. While I was there, I learnt about so many new ingredients and how to cook with them. I use pomegranate molasses all the time now – it's excellent for dressings. The street food in Lebanon is amazing, and these koftas are inspired by some I ate there. There was a particular 'hole in the wall' type of place that served warmed lamb flat breads straight from the oven at the end of my street. I would grab one of those and a large glass of deep pink, freshly made pomegranate juice for my breakfast. There were just so many amazing food options in Lebanon.*

2130 ENERGY KJ	513 ENERGY KCAL	28.9g PROTEIN	40.8g FAT	12.8g SATURATED FAT	9.5g CARBOHYDRATES	7.2g TOTAL SUGARS	1.3g FIBRE	1.6g SALT

SERVES 4

For the koftas

500g lamb mince

25g pine nuts

1 teaspoon ground coriander

1 teaspoon ground cumin

1 teaspoon dried oregano

2 garlic cloves, grated

½ teaspoon chilli powder

salt and freshly ground black pepper

For the Beirut chopped salad

½ cucumber, peeled and deseeded

8 radishes, diced

10 cherry tomatoes, halved

50ml extra virgin olive oil

20ml pomegranate molasses

1 teaspoon pickled wild thyme (if you can't get this, use marjoram)

For the tahini yogurt dip

4 tablespoons Greek yogurt

1 tablespoon tahini

1 teaspoon runny honey

juice of 1 lemon

First, mix all the kofta ingredients together in a bowl and season well. Shape into about twelve little balls, pop them on a plate, cover and refrigerate while you prepare the rest of the dish.

For the salad, cut the cucumber into cubes and place in a bowl with the radishes and cherry tomatoes. Add the olive oil, pomegranate molasses and thyme, season and mix well.

For the sauce, mix the yogurt, tahini, honey and lemon together and season.

When you are ready to eat, heat up a griddle pan over a high heat and grill the koftas until golden brown all round and slightly pink inside – this should take about 10 minutes.

Serve with the sauce and the salad.

Kale and turkey superfood salad with miso soy dressing

* * * *Although I believe you can boost your body and its immune system with good nutrition, it's a good idea to take the 'superfood' label with a pinch of salt and have a closer look at which foods are the real nutritional powerhouses. This salad is great, with curly kale (mega iron), turkey (low in fat, high in zinc and amino acids), pumpkin seeds (antioxidants) and baby spinach (even more iron!). The dressing is light in calories, but high in flavour.*

2459 ENERGY KJ	588 ENERGY KCAL	62.3g PROTEIN	31.3g FAT	8.1g SATURATED FAT	15.1g CARBOHYDRATES	11.5g TOTAL SUGARS	8.1g FIBRE	3g SALT

per 30g serving of Miso Soy Dressing

265 ENERGY KJ	64 ENERGY KCAL	1.4g PROTEIN	4.3g FAT	0.8g SATURATED FAT	4.4g CARBOHYDRATES	3.7g TOTAL SUGARS	0.3g FIBRE	0.7g SALT

SERVES 4

200g **curly kale, finely shredded**

100g **pousse** (**baby spinach**)

2 **avocados, peeled, stoned and sliced**

100g **spring onions, finely sliced**

200g **cooked beetroot, diced**

200g **carrots, grated**

200g **green beans, blanched and**
    chopped into 2.5cm pieces

100g **cucumber, diced**

150g **cherry tomatoes, halved**

800g **cooked turkey breast, shredded**

200g **breakfast radishes, finely sliced**

50g **pumpkin or sunflower seeds**

For the miso soy dressing

100ml **rice vinegar**

1 **tablespoon miso**

2 **tablespoons runny honey**

1 **tablespoon finely grated fresh ginger**

2 **tablespoons sesame oil**

1 **tablespoon groundnut oil**

1½ **teaspoons lime juice**

3 **tablespoons soy sauce**

1 **tablespoon English mustard**

Make the dressing by mixing all the dressing ingredients together in a small bowl. Any dressing that you don't use now will keep for a week or so.

In a large bowl, mix together the kale, baby spinach, avocados, spring onions, beetroot, carrots, beans, cucumber and cherry tomatoes with a tablespoonful of the dressing. Top with the turkey and radishes, then sprinkle with the pumpkin or sunflower seeds. Drizzle with about 1 teaspoon more of the dressing and serve.

Saffron and yogurt chicken and cauliflower rice salad with mint and herb sauce

✳✳✳ *Saffron and yogurt make a beautiful marinade for chicken, and the mint dressing lifts the dish at the end. Cauliflower rice is a relatively new fad, but I do love it. Tellingly, when you Google 'cauliflower' these days, 'cauliflower rice' pops up before 'cauliflower cheese'. Don't get me wrong, I do love the classic cauliflower cheese, but it is cool to see so many people getting into healthier food, too. Using veggies like cauliflower as a substitute for mainstream carbs is a great way to reduce your carb intake and get more vegetables in.*

2941 ENERGY KJ	707 ENERGY KCAL	55.7g PROTEIN	47.5g FAT	17.8g SATURATED FAT	15g CARBOHYDRATES	13.2g TOTAL SUGARS	4g FIBRE	1.6g SALT

SERVES 4

500g boneless chicken thighs, each chopped in half

For the marinade

2 tablespoons Greek yogurt

50ml boiling water

a large pinch of saffron threads

1 garlic clove, grated

For the mint and herb sauce

2 small handfuls of fresh coriander leaves

2 small handfuls of fresh mint leaves

240g Greek yogurt

For the cauliflower rice salad

1 cauliflower

100g pomegranate seeds

50ml olive oil

squeeze of lemon juice

2 spring onions, sliced

salt and freshly ground black pepper

To make the marinade, place the yogurt in a large bowl or dish. In a separate bowl, pour the boiling water over the saffron and let infuse for a few minutes before mixing with the yogurt. Add the garlic, mix well and then add the chicken. Coat the chicken in the mix and leave to marinate in the fridge – the longer the better, but make sure it's at least 1 hour.

Meanwhile, make the mint and herb sauce. Place the coriander and mint in a food processor along with the yogurt, and blitz into a bright green sauce.

Now move on to the cauliflower rice. Cut the hard core and stalks from the cauliflower and discard. Pulse the rest in a food processor until it forms rice-like grains. Tip these into a heatproof bowl and cover with clingfilm. Pierce the clingfilm, then microwave for 7 minutes on high – there is no need to add any water.

Mix the pomegranate seeds, olive oil, lemon juice and spring onions into the cauliflower rice and season.

Finally place a frying or griddle pan on a high heat and cook the chicken for 6–7 minutes on each side until cooked through. Serve with a big spoonful of the cauliflower rice and some sauce.

Burrata four ways

✱✱✱ Burrata is just such a gorgeous ingredient. It's a creamy cheese, with a slight acidity – essentially mozzarella injected with cream. At my restaurants, we try very hard to source the very best-quality burrata. It's growing increasingly popular and can now be found in lots of delis and supermarkets. Mozzarella can, of course, be used as a substitute, but do try to get burrata if you can – it's really worth seeking out. It has a very short shelf life, though, so eat it as soon as possible. Below are my four favourite ways with burrata.

Burrata with fennel, za'atar and pomegranate

1158 ENERGY KJ	280 ENERGY KCAL	16.4g PROTEIN	23.1g FAT	14.5g SATURATED FAT	1.5g CARBOHYDRATES	1.1g TOTAL SUGARS	0.6g FIBRE	0.5g SALT

SERVES 4

a large handful of finely chopped fennel

1 tablespoon finely chopped mint

2 tablespoons pomegranate seeds

4 x 120g mini burrata, drained

1 teaspoon za'atar (see page 151)

drizzle of good-quality extra virgin olive oil

sea salt and freshly ground black pepper

Simply mix the fennel, mint and pomegranate seeds together, then arrange on a plate with the burrata on the side. Sprinkle the burrata with the za'atar, drizzle with the oil and season. Serve!

Burrata with heirloom tomatoes and basil

2095 ENERGY KJ	507 ENERGY KCAL	16.8g PROTEIN	47.6g FAT	18.1g SATURATED FAT	3.1g CARBOHYDRATES	2.6g TOTAL SUGARS	1.1g FIBRE	0.5g SALT

SERVES 4

4–5 different-sized heirloom tomatoes

4 x 120g mini burrata

100ml good-quality extra virgin olive oil

1 tablespoon chopped baby basil

sea salt and freshly ground black pepper

This is really very easy – it's not cooking, but simply assembling the best possible ingredients. Firstly, allow the tomatoes to reach room temperature. When you're ready to eat, slice into all different shapes and sizes – I love to thinly slice the larger ones and lay them out as a foundation, then build it all up with the smaller ones. Drain the burrata off and place in the centre of the tomatoes. Drizzle with the oil, sprinkle with the basil, season and serve.

Burrata with speck and pickled cherries

1467 ENERGY KJ | 354 ENERGY KCAL | 22g PROTEIN | 27.4g FAT | 15.6g SATURATED FAT | 4.4g CARBOHYDRATES | 4.2g TOTAL SUGARS | 0.3g FIBRE | 1.5g SALT

per 100g serving of Pickled Cherries

170 ENERGY KJ | 40 ENERGY KCAL | 0.8g PROTEIN | 0.1g FAT | 0g SATURATED FAT | 8.4g CARBOHYDRATES | 8.3g TOTAL SUGARS | 0.6g FIBRE | 0.1g SALT

SERVES 4

4–8 very finely sliced pieces of speck

4 x 120g mini burrata, drained

200g Pickled Cherries (see below)

1 tablespoon very good extra virgin olive oil

salt and freshly ground black pepper

For the Pickled cherries

500g cherries, washed but with the stems and stones still in

200ml cider vinegar

50g sweetener (stevia is good)

1 sprig of thyme

a few cloves

a few black peppercorns

Begin by making the pickled cherries. Try to make these a few days before you want to use them – they're best after a week or so. Place the cherries in a heatproof bowl. Pour the vinegar into a saucepan with 200ml water and place over a medium heat. Add the sweetener, thyme, cloves and peppercorns. Simmer for about 5 minutes until the stevia has dissolved and then pour over the cherries. Either transfer to a sterilised jar (see page 184) and seal, or an airtight container. They will keep, refrigerated, for a few weeks.

When you're ready to serve, arrange the speck on some plates with the burrata and some of the pickled cherries. Drizzle with the olive oil and season, then serve.

Burrata with puntarelle and bottarga

2103 ENERGY KJ | 509 ENERGY KCAL | 18.5g PROTEIN | 48g FAT | 18.2g SATURATED FAT | 2g CARBOHYDRATES | 0.4g TOTAL SUGARS | 0.6g FIBRE | 0.8g SALT

SERVES 4

250g puntarelle stems with a few leaves, trimmed and finely sliced (if you can't get puntarelle, radicchio is a good alternative)

100g good-quality olive oil

4 x 120g mini burrata, drained

50g bottarga (see page 128), finely sliced, plus extra for grating

salt and freshly ground black pepper

Place the puntarelle in a bowl with the olive oil. Season with salt and pepper and mix together.

Transfer to a plate and arrange the burrata on the side. Top with the sliced bottarga and finely grate over some more. Serve!

Tuna seaweed poke

★★☆ *I LOVE THIS DISH!! Partly because of the name (who doesn't love a good poke?! Although it's actually pronounced 'poh-key'). But I also love the flavours and ingredients. It is from Hawaii, and is normally served on rice, but works really well without it, too. I tried this dish in LA and it feels modern and tasty. You can experiment a little with this one. I like a bit of chilli, but it isn't always included. The seaweed is important, though, as it makes it different from a ceviche or carpaccio and it adds cartloads of iron and nutrients.*

1090 ENERGY KJ	260 ENERGY KCAL	32.5g PROTEIN	13.1g FAT	2.9g SATURATED FAT	3.8g CARBOHYDRATES	3.2g TOTAL SUGARS	3.6g FIBRE	4.7g SALT

SERVES 4

500g super-fresh tuna fillet, diced into perfect 1cm cubes

4 spring onions, sliced

1 teaspoon sesame seeds

2 nori seaweed sheets, finely sliced into short julienne

1 teaspoon wasabi tobiko (optional)

1 avocado, peeled, stoned and diced

edible flower petals, to garnish

Spiced Soy Seaweed Crisps (page 179), 3 per serving

For the dressing

½ tablespoon sesame oil

50ml soy sauce

½ teaspoon grated fresh ginger

pinch of chilli powder

½ teaspoon lime zest

squeeze of lime juice

Mix the dressing ingredients together in a small bowl.

In a large bowl, mix together the tuna, spring onions, sesame seeds, nori and wasabi tobiko, if using, and mix well. Pour over the dressing and mix well again. Finally, add the avocado.

Serve the poke layered up with the Spiced Soy Seaweed Crisps and edible flower petals.

Chef's tip: *Wasabi tobiko is flying fish roe flavoured with wasabi. It really packs a punch of flavour and is great for ceviches etc.*

Crudo four ways

Salmon ceviche with avocado and crab

★★☆ *This uses the same dressing as the scallop carpaccio opposite, but, with the addition of avocado and crab, the end result is quite different. The salmon is much more robust than the scallops, and it can take more dressing, too.*

1426 ENERGY KJ	341 ENERGY KCAL	42.7g PROTEIN	18.2g FAT	3.4g SATURATED FAT	1.7g CARBOHYDRATES	1g TOTAL SUGARS	1.8g FIBRE	0.8g SALT

SERVES 4

2 avocados

juice of 1 lime

16 slices super-fresh salmon

200g picked white crabmeat

a small handful of micro cress

Yuzu Dressing (see page 182)

salt and freshly ground black pepper

avocado oil, to serve

Place the avocados in a high-powered blender and blitz until extremely smooth. Stir in the lime juice and season.

Take out four plates. Lay four slices of salmon on each plate, then pipe or drop on some little dollops of the avocado mixture. Sprinkle over the crab and cress, and finally drizzle over a generous amount of dressing (maybe 2 dessertspoons per plate). Finish with drops of avocado oil and serve.

Sea bass carpaccio with sumac, lemon and pomegranate

★★☆ *Beirut has been called the Paris of the Middle East for years and as soon as the troubles die down (however sporadically this lasts) the city reverts back to high glamour. There is a certain zest for life that I haven't seen anywhere else, and I sadly suppose it is because the Lebanese have realised how delicate the siuation can be. When I lived there in 2010, we would spend the weekend in glitzy beach clubs, and this dish is inspired by one of my favourite beach club lunches, where they would prep fresh fish in front of you and serve it.*

1476 ENERGY KJ	356 ENERGY KCAL	17.2g PROTEIN	30.5g FAT	4.4g SATURATED FAT	3.5g CARBOHYDRATES	3.3g TOTAL SUGARS	1.2g FIBRE	0.7g SALT

SERVES 4

2 sea bass fillets (about 150g each)

1 lemon

1 teaspoon sumac

25g pistachios, chopped

100g pomegranate seeds

100ml extra virgin olive oil

sea salt crystals, to serve

Slice the sea bass super thinly and arrange on four plates. Then segment the lemon so that you just have the flesh and no pith or skin. Arrange the lemon segments on top of the sea bass. Sprinkle with the sumac, pistachios and pomegranate seeds, then drizzle with the oil. Finish off with some sea salt crystals and serve.

Scallop carpaccio with yuzu, fennel and mandarin

✭✭✭ *This dish is all about the freshness and beauty of the scallops. At Pont St, we get our scallops from Ethical Shellfish on the Isle of Mull. They are fully alive when they arrive, and the flesh is firm and sweet. I love this dish in the summer.*

528 ENERGY KJ | 126 ENERGY KCAL | 15.3g PROTEIN | 4.8g FAT | 0.8g SATURATED FAT | 5.8g CARBOHYDRATES | 3.5g TOTAL SUGARS | 2.1g FIBRE | 0.3g SALT

SERVES 4

12 diver-caught scallops in the shell, alive and kicking

2 baby fennel bulbs, finely sliced

2 mandarins, segmented

1 tablespoon extra virgin olive oil

Yuzu dressing (see page 182)

1 teaspoon baby basil

salt and freshly ground black pepper

Carefully take the scallops out of their shells and remove the corals. Gently wash off any sand and set aside.

Place the fennel in a bowl with the mandarin segments. Drizzle over a touch of olive oil and season with salt and pepper.

Slice the scallops thinly and place on plates. Arrange the fennel and mandarins on top and then pour over a good amount of the dressing. Add a few more drops of olive oil and finish with the basil.

Beef carpaccio, wild mushrooms, watercress and Parmesan

✭✭✭ *This is a bit of a classic combo that still feels chic to me. Wild mushrooms are at their best in autumn, and this is a really autumnal dish.*

1053 ENERGY KJ | 252 ENERGY KCAL | 33.5g PROTEIN | 12.8g FAT | 6.2g SATURATED FAT | 0.6g CARBOHYDRATES | 0.4g TOTAL SUGARS | 1.9g FIBRE | 0.4g SALT

SERVES 4

500g beef fillet from a good-quality butcher

1 teaspoon olive oil

300g mixed wild mushrooms, any dirt brushed off

150g watercress

Truffle Dressing (page 182)

50g Parmesan cheese shavings

salt and freshly ground black pepper

Trim the beef fillet and cut lengthways down the middle to give you two long sausage-shaped fillets of beef. Season heavily. Place in a pan over a very high heat and seal for a few minutes on each side. You want it coloured on the outside, but completely raw on the inside. Leave to cool and roll it in clingfilm, then place in the freezer.

Place a frying pan over a high heat and add the oil. Add the mushrooms in batches and cook until really golden brown, then season and take out to cool.

Take the beef out of the freezer and slice thinly with a sharp knife. Arrange the slices prettily on a plate. In a bowl, mix together the mushrooms and watercress with a touch of dressing, then lay on top of the beef. Finally, scatter over the Parmesan and serve.

Chicken liver, pomegranate, butternut squash and radicchio salad

★★☆ *Pomegranate molasses is really good for glazing meats. It has a sweet and sour flavour, a bit like aged balsamic. It's wonderful on chicken livers, which are high in iron and quick to cook. This is a flavour combination found a lot in the Middle East, which is where the inspiration for this dish lies. If you use the ready-peeled and chopped squash that you can get in most supermarkets, it makes this really speedy to prepare. To me this dish screams festive times – the deep purples, reds and oranges are all warming and beautiful.*

1205 ENERGY KJ	288 ENERGY KCAL	23.7g PROTEIN	15.6g FAT	2.7g SATURATED FAT	14.2g CARBOHYDRATES	10.7g TOTAL SUGARS	4g FIBRE	1.5g SALT

SERVES 4

300g butternut squash, peeled, deseeded and cut into wedges (or use ready-peeled and chopped)

50ml extra virgin olive oil, plus extra for drizzling

500g free-range chicken livers, trimmed

1 tablespoon pomegranate molasses

a pinch of sumac

2 small heads of radicchio, leaves torn

200g pomegranate seeds

sea salt and freshly ground black pepper

Preheat the oven to 200°C/gas mark 6.

Season the squash with salt and pepper, drizzle with some olive oil and place on a baking tray. Roast for 30 minutes, or until softened and golden.

Place a frying pan over a high heat and add the oil. Season the livers and add to the pan. Cook for about 3–4 minutes on each side (I like mine quite pink). Then add the pomegranate molasses and sumac.

When cooked, arrange the squash and torn radicchio leaves on a serving platter, then place the livers on top. Finally, sprinkle with the pomegranate seeds and serve.

Barbecue chicken, blue cheese and pickled celery salad

★★☆ *What can I say? I wanted those classic American flavours, but without the junk food guilt. This is how I achieved it: grilled barbecue sauce-glazed chicken, creamy blue cheese and crisp celery. All these flavours are real classics and shine through.*

2060 ENERGY KJ	493 ENERGY KCAL	43g PROTEIN	31.8g FAT	13.5g SATURATED FAT	8.5g CARBOHYDRATES	7.9g TOTAL SUGARS	0.6g FIBRE	3.1g SALT

SERVES 4

8 boneless, skinless chicken thighs

50ml olive oil

1 tablespoon barbecue sauce

150ml white wine vinegar

50g sugar (any type will do)

4 celery sticks, thinly sliced, plus celery leaves to garnish

½ iceberg lettuce

200g Saint Agur blue cheese, crumbled

salt and freshly ground black pepper

Classic Dressing (see page 68), to serve (optional)

For the spice mix

1 teaspoon smoked paprika

½ teaspoon garlic salt

½ teaspoon ground cumin

½ teaspoon ground coriander

¼ teaspoon ground turmeric

½ teaspoon ground allspice

pinch of dried thyme

pinch of dried oregano

First make the spice mix. Mix all the spices together in a bowl, then rub the mix into the chicken thighs, along with the oil. Season with salt and pepper.

Heat a griddle pan over a high heat, or get a barbecue ready. When hot enough, cook the chicken thighs for about 5–7 minutes on each side or until cooked through, depending on how thick they are. Work in batches if necessary. Take off the heat and brush the thighs with the barbecue sauce. Set aside.

Now pickle the celery. Place the vinegar and sugar in a saucepan and heat over a medium heat for 5 minutes. Pour over the sliced celery in a bowl and leave for at least 1 hour in the fridge, preferably longer.

When you're ready to serve, break up the iceberg lettuce leaves into large pieces and arrange on a platter or plate. Then slice the chicken and arrange on top, along with the blue cheese, pickled celery and celery leaves. If you wish, drizzle with Classic Dressing, but it's just as delicious without, as the pickled celery gives a real kick of flavour.

Venison, duck and chicken terrine

✳✳✳ *Shop-bought pâtés and terrines can contain all sorts of unwanted ingredients, so make your own with these simple, pure ingredients. You can make it with just pork and chicken if game is not your thing, but game meat is generally full of flavour and low in fat, so works well for terrines. It might seem strange that a terrine could be eaten in a diet, but actually, as long as you make it yourself, they are great for a lunch or starter.*

1176 ENERGY KJ	283 ENERGY KCAL	17.4g PROTEIN	21.7g FAT	8.9g SATURATED FAT	4.4g CARBOHYDRATES	2g TOTAL SUGARS	0.7g FIBRE	1.9g SALT

SERVES 15

300g smoked streaky bacon slices

100g butter

2 garlic cloves, chopped

2 banana shallots, diced

pinch each of ground nutmeg
    and mace

500g minced pork

250g venison mince

250g free-range chicken liver,
    trimmed and diced

50g pistachios

25ml brandy

½ teaspoon each of sea salt and
    freshly ground black pepper

1 skinless duck breast, cut into strips

1 skinless chicken breast, cut
    into strips

Preheat the oven to 160°C/gas mark 3. Neatly line a classic-sized terrine tin with the streaky bacon. Make sure that the bacon hangs over the edge of the tin.

Place a frying pan over a medium heat. Add the butter and fry the garlic, shallots, nutmeg and mace in the butter until the shallots are translucent. Transfer to a large bowl with the pork, venison, chicken livers, pistachios, brandy and salt and pepper and mix well. Press half of this mixture into the bacon-lined terrine. Now lay the duck and chicken breast strips down the middle so that you have a layer of pure meat. Next, press the rest of the mince mixture in – it should come to about 1cm above the top of the tin, to allow for shrinkage. Fold the excess bacon over the top.

Cover with the terrine lid or some foil and place the terrine tin in a deep baking tray. Fill the tray with water so that it reaches halfway up the sides of the tin and place in the oven for 1½ hours.

Remove the terrine from the tray of water and leave to cool slightly. Cut a piece of cardboard so that it fits snugly on top of the terrine. Weight it down with food cans to press and leave the terrine overnight in the fridge.

The next day, place a chopping board on the work surface. Run a knife around the outside of the tin, then carefully lever the terrine out and onto the board. Clean up some of the excess fat and jelly, then rewrap the terrine in clingfilm and pop back in the fridge. When you are ready to eat, serve a slice with some lovely wholegrain mustard and a dressed green salad.

Dorset crab and white asparagus with white balsamic and honey dressing

✱✳✳ *This is a very simple supper. I'm attracted to the pale white and cream hues of the asparagus and crab. White asparagus is great and you can buy it raw when in season, but more often than not, I grab a jar in my local deli and use it for quick but chic salads.*

1412 ENERGY KJ	341 ENERGY KCAL	24.9g PROTEIN	26g FAT	3.7g SATURATED FAT	1.6g CARBOHYDRATES	1.4g TOTAL SUGARS	0.5g FIBRE	1.9g SALT

SERVES 4

100g brown crabmeat

2 tablespoons Homemade
    Mayonnaise (see below)

pinch of cayenne pepper

1 teaspoon lemon zest

400g white crabmeat

lemon juice, to taste

150g wild rocket

1 x 200g jar white asparagus spears,
    drained

salt and freshly ground black pepper

For the dressing

20ml white balsamic vinegar

½ teaspoon runny honey

50ml extra virgin olive oil

In a bowl, mix together the brown crabmeat, mayonnaise, cayenne and lemon zest.

In a separate bowl, dress the white crabmeat with a touch of lemon juice and season.

Whisk the dressing ingredients together in a small bowl, then toss with the rocket in a larger bowl.

Take out four plates and spread some of the mayonnaise mixture on each one. Pile the rocket, white crabmeat and asparagus on top, then serve.

Homemade mayonnaise

Place **2 pasteurised egg yolks** and a **splash of white wine vinegar** in a blender and whizz for a few minutes until light and frothy. With the blender still running, gradually pour in **75ml vegetable oil** and **25ml extra virgin olive oil**. Continue to blend until the mixture is really thick and creamy, then stir in **1 teaspoon lemon juice** . Taste for seasoning and adjust if necessary.

Mezcal-cured salmon with avocado salsa

★★☆ *It's amazing how much I seem to sneak alcohol into my food! Ha ha ha. Sometimes it can be very interesting, though – the smokiness of the mezcal in the salmon cure here really works. Curing fish is an unusual yet simple way to prepare it, and you can use all sorts of flavours. I have cured using whisky, sake and vanilla, or just plain brown sugar and sea salt. I made this dish for Taste of London (a London-based food festival that showcases the best of London's restaurants) and it went down a bomb.*

1573 ENERGY KJ	377 ENERGY KCAL	26.7g PROTEIN	23.6g FAT	4.4g SATURATED FAT	16.2g CARBOHYDRATES	14.6g TOTAL SUGARS	3g FIBRE	1.4g SALT

SERVES 4
200g golden caster sugar
200g salt
zest of 1 lime
50ml mezcal
500g salmon fillet

For the avocado salsa
2 avocados, peeled, stoned and cut into 1cm dice
1 mango, peeled, stoned and cut into 1cm dice
½ red onion, finely diced
½ teaspoon chipotle paste
juice of 1 lime
salt and freshly ground black pepper

To garnish
6 breakfast radishes, finely sliced
a handful of fresh coriander leaves

Start at least 24 hours before you want to eat the salmon. Mix the sugar, salt, lime zest and mezcal together. Cut the salmon into two pieces. Place one piece on a plate, skin-side down, then spread the salty mix on top. Cover with the other piece of salmon, flesh-side down (so skin side out). Cover and leave in the fridge for 24–48 hours to cure.

When you are ready to plate and eat, make the avocado salsa by mixing together all the ingredients in a bowl.

Remove the salmon from the fridge and wash off the salt mix. Finely slice the salmon and lay the slices on four plates. Top with the salsa and garnish with the radishes and the coriander leaves.

Main Meals

Roasted chicken thighs with artichokes and chorizo

★☆☆ *This is an easy, simple supper dish for mid-week eats. Not everything can be cheffy, and this is low on time and planning and high on flavour. In my restaurants everything is prepped by hand, but I feel no shame in using canned artichokes at home. Chicken thighs have a good flavour and are easy to find, too. This is great served with the Caponata on page 140 or the Celeriac Mash on page 151.*

2097 ENERGY KJ	503 ENERGY KCAL	46.4g PROTEIN	34.2g FAT	9g SATURATED FAT	3g CARBOHYDRATES	1.6 TOTAL SUGARS	0.2g FIBRE	2g SALT

SERVES 4

600g boneless, skinless chicken thighs

150g mini chorizo, kept whole (if you can't get mini chorizo, use standard chorizo, crumbled or sliced)

4 garlic cloves

sprinkling of thyme leaves

1 x 400g can artichoke hearts

2 lemons, halved

50ml extra virgin olive oil

sea salt and freshly ground black pepper

Preheat the oven to 200°C/gas mark 6.

Place the chicken and chorizo in a roasting tray, then smash the garlic and add to the tray, along with the thyme leaves.

Drain off the artichokes, tear them in half and scatter them over the chicken. Squeeze the lemons over the top, then add the squeezed halves to the tray. Drizzle over the oil, season and mix everything together using your hands. Wash your hands thoroughly, then place the tray in the oven and cook for 30–40 minutes. Give it a stir halfway through to spread those lovely chorizo juices and then pop back in.

When golden and roasted, remove from the oven and serve with a pile of veggies or a salad.

Chicken paillard with honey, chilli and fennel marinade

★★☆ *Chicken can be a bit boring, but this marinade is one of my favourites. The fennel and chilli give it spice and depth of flavour, the lemon and white wine add acidity and the honey gives the whole thing a sweet glaze. It's quick to cook and easy, too. The sweet butternut squash and deep green vegetables make the perfect accompaniments.*

1930 ENERGY KJ	462 ENERGY KCAL	31.4g PROTEIN	30.8g FAT	5.1g SATURATED FAT	16.3g CARBOHYDRATES	10.9g TOTAL SUGARS	2.8g FIBRE	1.4g SALT

SERVES 4

4 free-range skinless chicken breasts

1 medium butternut squash, peeled, deseeded and cut into wedges

1 tablespoon olive oil

1 bunch of tenderstem broccoli

salt and freshly ground black pepper

For the marinade

15ml white wine

100ml extra virgin olive oil

½ teaspoon fennel seeds

½ teaspoon dried chilli flakes

½ teaspoon dried oregano

25ml runny honey

2 garlic cloves, roughly chopped

zest and juice of ½ lemon, plus wedges or halves to serve

½ teaspoon sea salt

Preheat the oven to 200°C/gas mark 6.

Cut an incision into the thickest part of the chicken breasts, and open up to a 'butterfly' shape. Place between two sheets of clingfilm and beat with a rolling pin or meat tenderiser until very flat.

In a bowl, mix together all the marinade ingredients. Set aside half, and add the chicken breasts to the bowl with the other half. Stir to coat, cover and place in the fridge while you roast the squash.

Place the prepared squash on a baking tray, drizzle with the oil and season. Roast for 30–40 minutes until golden brown.

Place a griddle pan over a high heat and get it nice and hot. When the squash has 8–10 minutes left, pop the chicken onto the griddle pan and cook for about 5 minutes on each side until cooked through and nice and charred on the outside – this will vary depending on thickness, so keep an eye on it. Add the lemon wedges or halves to the griddle pan too, to char.

Meanwhile, place the remaining marinade in a saucepan over a medium heat and bring to the boil. In a separate saucepan, cook the broccoli in boiling water for about 4 minutes before draining.

When everything is ready, plate up the squash, chicken and broccoli, and drizzle with the heated marinade. Serve with an extra wedge of charred lemon.

Crisp duck wings with miso glaze and kimchi salad

✶✶✶ *Deep-fried chicken wings are on every menu now, it seems. I was recently in NYC at a Californian-inspired restaurant called Uplands and had a really interesting dish of deep-fried duck wings, which I loved! This is my version of it. I have confited the duck wings, then prepared a sweet miso glaze. The piquant kimchi adds balance.*

1010 ENERGY KJ	243 ENERGY KCAL	15.7g PROTEIN	17.2g FAT	5.3g SATURATED FAT	6.2g CARBOHYDRATES	4.4g TOTAL SUGARS	1.1g FIBRE	1.9g SALT

SERVES 4

12 duck wings, halved and tips removed

400g duck fat

salt and freshly ground black pepper

For the miso glaze

2 tablespoons white miso

1 tablespoon runny honey

1 teaspoon soy sauce

1 tablespoon mirin (a sweet Chinese rice wine)

For the kimchi salad

1 Chinese cabbage, cut into medium strips and core discarded

2 carrots, cut into strips

100g salt (this is washed off after)

1 teaspoon fish sauce

1 tablespoon gochujang paste

2.5cm piece fresh ginger, finely chopped

1 garlic clove, finely crushed

a bunch of spring onions, finely chopped

Preheat the oven to 150°C/gas mark 2. Place the duck wings in a medium-sized deep baking dish, season and cover with the duck fat. Then cover the dish with foil and place in the oven for about 1½ hours.

Meanwhile, make the kimchi salad. Place the cabbage in a bowl with the carrots and salt and mix together. Leave for 30 minutes, then wash off the salt and squeeze out any water from the vegetables.

In a separate bowl, mix together the fish sauce, gochujang paste, ginger and garlic. Now add the cabbage and carrot mix, along with the spring onions. Mix well and leave to sit for at least 30 minutes before serving. You can make this the day before if you prefer, to allow the flavours to develop further.

When the wings are cooked and tender, take them out of the fat. Be careful, as it will be hot! Set aside on a large baking tray.

To make the glaze, mix the miso, honey, soy sauce and mirin together in a small saucepan, season with black pepper and simmer over a medium heat for 2 minutes. Take off the heat and leave to cool.

Preheat the grill to very high. Brush the duck wings with the miso glaze and grill on all sides until golden and crisp. Serve with the kimchi salad.

Roasted duck breast on beluga lentils with balsamic onions and pine nuts

★★✫ *Duck is one of my favourite meats, but a lot of people don't like it because they think it's too fatty. I don't have a problem with fat (unless it's on my hips!), and if you cook the duck as I explain here, most of the fat is rendered and crisped up. I serve the duck with some beluga lentils – I love their nuttiness, and you can even buy them pre-cooked these days if cooking pulses scares you.*

2061 ENERGY KJ	493 ENERGY KCAL	41.9g PROTEIN	27.2g FAT	4.8g SATURATED FAT	20.5g CARBOHYDRATES	3.2g TOTAL SUGARS	5.6g FIBRE	1.2g SALT

SERVES 4

4 duck breasts (about 150–180g each)

50ml olive oil

2 onions, sliced into 1 cm rings

50g pine nuts

a sprig of thyme, leaves picked

100ml balsamic vinegar

150g curly kale

400g cooked beluga lentils

salt and freshly ground black pepper

Preheat the oven to 200°C/gas mark 6. Trim the excess fat from the edges of the duck breasts and then score the skin in a criss-cross pattern. Season with salt and pepper.

Put a frying pan over a low to medium heat and place the duck breasts in the pan, skin-side down. Cook for about 10 minutes to render the fat and crisp up the skin. Moderate and change the temperature when needed so that it doesn't get burnt. Drain the fat off as you go. Towards the end, increase the heat and brown the skin for the last 2 minutes, then flip over and seal on the flesh side.

Transfer to a roasting tray and roast for 4 minutes – you don't want it overcooked; pink is best. Then take it out and set it aside to rest.

Heat the olive oil in the same frying pan you cooked the duck in, and add the onions. Cook them for about 10 minutes until softened – try not to burn them. Add the pine nuts and thyme leaves and fry for another 2 minutes, then add the balsamic and cook for 5 more minutes.

Meanwhile, place a saucepan of water on to boil. Add the kale and simmer for 4 minutes, then drain. At the same time, heat up the lentils in a smaller saucepan.

When you are ready to eat, slice the duck breasts, and place each one on a plate with some lentils and kale. Spoon over the onion mixture and serve.

Low-carb dim sum

★★★ *Dim sum is something I crave constantly, but when I am trying to cut down on starch and sugar in my diet, it doesn't really fit in with my eating plan. Below are some of my totally inauthentic versions, but they do give you the feeling of dim sum and it's really fun experimenting with them. I love the windows in London's Chinatown with all the glistening deep red pork and golden roast ducks hanging up. The little pork cheeks are inspired by those Chinatown roast meats. I braise the cheeks in smoky Lapsang Souchong tea and star anise to give them a real depth of flavour, then glaze them with a sweet, spicy glaze – they are really moreish. The pork cheeks also leave behind a beautiful stock, which I strain off to use as a base for soups. Bean curd wraps are high in protein and really useful for dim sum. Yes, they're an uncommon ingredient, but well worth sourcing, as they are so versatile. They also deep-fry well, but I am not supposed to tell you that...*

Lapsang-braised pork cheeks with five-spice glaze

1418 ENERGY KJ	338 ENERGY KCAL	46.9g PROTEIN	11.2g FAT	4.1g SATURATED FAT	15.9g CARBOHYDRATES	11.2g TOTAL SUGARS	2.7g FIBRE	1.5g SALT

SERVES 4

1 litre vegetable stock

2 tablespoons Lapsang Souchong tea leaves

2 star anise

4 pork cheeks

For the glaze

1 teaspoon Chinese five-spice powder

1 tablespoon runny honey

1 teaspoon dark soy sauce

1 teaspoon hoisin sauce

To make the braising liquor, place the stock, tea leaves and star anise in a large saucepan and bring to the boil. Drop in the pork cheeks and simmer, covered, for 1 hour.

Preheat the oven to 200°C/gas mark 6.

Remove the pork cheeks from the liquor with a slotted spoon and set aside.

In a bowl, mix together all the glaze ingredients and then add the pork cheeks, stirring to coat.

Place the cheeks on a baking tray and roast for 30 minutes until beautifully glazed and golden, basting with the glaze as you go.

Serve with chilli oil, greens and the Pork, Prawn and Shiitake Bean Curd Wraps (see opposite).

Pork, prawn and shiitake bean curd wraps

850 ENERGY KJ | 203 ENERGY KCAL | 18.5g PROTEIN | 6g FAT | 1.4g SATURATED FAT | 16.2g CARBOHYDRATES | 3g TOTAL SUGARS | 0.1g FIBRE | 2.1g SALT

SERVES 4

4 dried shiitake mushrooms

150g pork mince

**100g shelled raw king prawns,
    finely chopped**

5cm piece of fresh ginger, grated

2 spring onions, finely chopped

**1 tablespoon Chinese rice wine
    (or sherry)**

2 tablespoons light soy sauce

1 teaspoon cornflour

2 sheets bean curd

salt and freshly ground black pepper

For the sauce

50ml sweet sherry

2 tablespoons light soy sauce

1 teaspoon cornflour

Begin by making the filling. Soak the shiitake mushrooms in a bowl of freshly boiled water for 10 minutes, then drain and retain 100ml of the soaking water. Chop the mushrooms up and place in a large mixing bowl. Add the pork mince and prawns and mix together. Stir in the ginger, spring onions, Chinese rice wine (or sherry) and soy sauce, and sprinkle over the cornflour. Season and mix well.

Boil the kettle and place the bean curd sheets in a baking tray. Pour the boiled water over the sheets and soak for 1 minute, then carefully drain off the water. Spread the sheets out separately onto a clean work surface. Take the filling and place it in a sausage shape about 2.5cm wide in the middle of each sheet. Roll up the wrappers tightly to make two large sausage shapes. Then chop each one into pieces about 10cm long.

There are two ways to cook these: you can either bake or steam them. To bake, preheat the oven to 200°C/gas mark 6. Place the wraps in a baking tray, cover with foil and roast for 10 minutes. To steam, place in a double-layer bamboo steamer over a pan of boiling water for 10 minutes.

Meanwhile, make the sauce. Place the retained mushroom soaking water in a small saucepan with the sherry and light soy sauce. Mix together and simmer over a low heat for 10 minutes. In a small bowl, mix the cornflour with a touch of water and whisk in to the pan to thicken the sauce.

When the dim sum is cooked, transfer to a serving plate then pour over the sauce. Serve with chilli oil, steamed Chinese greens and the Lapsang-Braised Pork Cheeks (see opposite).

Honey- and mustard-glazed gammon with Waldorf slaw

★★☆ *You can fall into the trap of living on cold cuts when following a high-protein diet. Baking your own hams is far superior to buying shop-bought, so give it a try. As a baked ham has something of a celebration feel to it, this is a good recipe to have up your sleeve. I use it at Christmas, with the addition of cloves. The Waldorf slaw served with the ham is my take on Waldorf Salad. I miss out the mayonnaise and just have the wonderful crispness of the celery and apple, and the crunch of the nuts. This slaw is also perfect with roast pork.*

1910 ENERGY KJ	459 ENERGY KCAL	45.6g PROTEIN	26.8g FAT	7.2g SATURATED FAT	8.7g CARBOHYDRATES	8.4g TOTAL SUGARS	1.6g FIBRE	5.7g SALT

SERVES 4–7

1.5kg gammon joint

For the glaze

1 tablespoon runny honey

1 tablespoon demerara sugar

1 tablespoon English mustard powder

For the Waldorf slaw

6 celery sticks, finely sliced on the diagonal

3 apples, cored and chopped into thin strips

50g walnuts, roughly chopped

1 tablespoon Classic Dressing (see page 68)

Place the gammon in a large saucepan. Add enough water to cover it and place over a medium heat. Bring to the boil, then reduce the heat and simmer, partly covered, for 20 minutes.

Preheat the oven to 180°C/gas mark 4.

Remove the ham from the water and place on a baking tray. To make the glaze, mix the ingredients together in a bowl. Spread or pour this mixture over the ham, rubbing or brushing it into all the nooks and crannies. Now pop the ham in the oven for 1 hour 15 minutes, or until nicely caramelised and brown.

To make the slaw, simply mix the celery, apple and walnuts together in a bowl, then dress with the Classic Dressing. Serve alongside the ham, thickly sliced.

Moussaka-stuffed aubergine

★★☆ *My family have lived in Greece for 15 years and I love the food out there. Moussaka is one of those iconic dishes: layers of cinnamon-rich lamb and tomato, creamy cheese sauce and tender aubergine. I have adapted it for this diet by serving the meat inside the aubergine, and replacing the heavy béchamel sauce with a low-carb alternative made with Greek yogurt, eggs and cheese. I like to serve this with the Beiruti salad on page 75.*

3248 ENERGY KJ	781 ENERGY KCAL	49.1g PROTEIN	56.5g FAT	26.1g SATURATED FAT	16.3g CARBOHYDRATES	12.7g TOTAL SUGARS	3.1g FIBRE	2.8g SALT

SERVES 4

2 large aubergines

50ml olive oil

2 onions, finely diced

4 garlic cloves, finely crushed

500g lamb mince

½ teaspoon dried chilli flakes

1 teaspoon ground cinnamon

100ml red wine (optional)

400g can chopped tomatoes

400ml vegetable stock

½ teaspoon dried oregano

1 bay leaf

salt and freshly ground black pepper

For the topping

600g full-fat Greek yogurt

2 free-range egg yolks

150g Parmesan cheese, grated

Cut the aubergines in half. Score around the edges, then score the cut side in a criss-cross pattern and spoon out the insides so that you are left with four aubergine 'boats' or shells. If you like, you can set the aubergine flesh aside and add it to the lamb mixture later.

Place a frying pan over a medium heat and add the oil. Add the onions and cook for a few minutes, then add the garlic and mince (and aubergine flesh, if using), along with the chilli flakes and cinnamon. Continue frying to get some colour, breaking up the mince and stirring all the while so that you don't burn the onions and garlic.

When the lamb is browned, add the wine (if using), tomatoes and vegetable stock. Bring it to the boil and season, then add the oregano and bay leaf and simmer, uncovered, for 40 minutes.

Now preheat the oven to 180°C/gas mark 4 and place the aubergine shells on a baking tray.

In a bowl, mix together the yogurt and egg yolks, and season.

Divide the lamb mixture between the aubergine shells, then top with the yogurt and egg mixture. Finally, sprinkle over the cheese.

Bake for 30 minutes, then serve with a salad.

Slow-roasted coconut spiced pork in lettuce wraps

✴✴✴ *I travelled to Bali with my family for the first time at the age of 12. It was such an eye-opener for me and the dishes I saw there have stayed with me ever since. If you head up to the centre of the island to Ubud, they have an amazing place that cooks suckling pig with all these beautiful aromatic flavours and spices. I've been back many times since, and it's one of those meal experiences that you dream of. This is my miniature, London kitchen-friendly version.*

2344 ENERGY KJ	562 ENERGY KCAL	58.1g PROTEIN	33.9g FAT	19.5g SATURATED FAT	6.5g CARBOHYDRATES	5.6g TOTAL SUGARS	1.4g FIBRE	1.2g SALT

SERVES 4

1kg pork shoulder

½ cucumber, cut into batons

1 iceberg lettuce, separated into
   large leaves

a small handful of mint leaves, torn

50g peanuts, roughly chopped

drizzle of chilli sauce (optional)

salt and freshly ground black pepper

For the marinade

200ml coconut cream

2 red chillies

1 lemongrass stalk

5cm piece fresh ginger

1 teaspoon lime zest, plus extra
   if needed

½ teaspoon coriander seeds

½ teaspoon mixed peppercorns

Preheat the oven to 150°C/gas mark 2.

Place all the marinade ingredients in a food processor and blitz together until smooth. Then rub the mixture into the pork shoulder and season well. Place on a baking tray and cover with foil. Place in the oven and cook for at least 2 hours, but up to 4. For the last 15 minutes of the cooking time, remove the foil and increase the heat to 200°C/gas mark 6.

When the pork is ready, remove from the oven and leave until it's cool enough to handle, then tear it into shreds. Transfer to a bowl with all the juices from the baking tray and mix together. Season and add another few shavings of lime zest at this point to make the flavour pop out.

To serve, layer up the pork and cucumber in the lettuce leaves, then sprinkle with the mint and peanuts. Add a touch of chilli sauce if you want, but beware, it contains sugar!

Roast beef, celeriac gratin, wild mushrooms and charred onions

✳✳✳ *Anyone who knows me is aware that my Sundays are sacred. They revolve around cooking, eating and, sometimes, a fair bit of drinking. This is my chef's diet version of a Sunday roast, and it's got all the elements I want. It has earthy, deep flavours, with creamy gratin, rare beef and roasted onions. After a 60-hour working week of jam-packed days and eating on the go, this is the BOMB. Make sure you get a really good bit of beef. Use the leftovers to make my Roast Beef, Red Onion, Roasted Squash and Blue Cheese Radicchio Wraps (page 72).*

3077 ENERGY KJ	739 ENERGY KCAL	83.8g PROTEIN	41.9g FAT	21.6g SATURATED FAT	6.3g CARBOHYDRATES	4.2g TOTAL SUGARS	3.3g FIBRE	1.1g SALT

SERVES 4

3 teaspoons olive oil

1.5kg rib of beef

2 sweet white onions, peeled

200g mixed wild mushrooms

2 garlic cloves, sliced

1 tablespoon roughly chopped
    flat-leaf parsley

For the gratin

2 celeriacs, peeled and finely sliced
    using a mandolin or sharp knife

100ml vegetable stock

25ml double cream

1 sprig of thyme

2 garlic cloves, peeled but left whole

sea salt and freshly ground
    black pepper

For the shallot purée

8 banana shallots, chopped

50g butter

1 sprig of thyme

25ml double cream

Preheat the oven to 200°C/gas mark 6.

Begin with the gratin. Place the sliced celeriac in a bowl. Pour the stock and cream into a saucepan along with the thyme and garlic and place over a medium heat to warm through. Pour the heated mixture over the celeriac and season heavily.

Take a 20cm square baking tin and line with greaseproof paper, then start layering up the coated celeriac slices. Continue layering until you have used them all up – the gratin should be about 5cm deep when you're finished. Cover with foil and place in the oven. Cook for 40–60 minutes until a skewer can easily be inserted. Remove the foil for the last 10 minutes to colour the top a bit.

Remove the gratin from the oven and keep warm until ready to eat. (I like to press it, cool it completely, then remove it from the tin and cut it into different shapes before reheating and serving just to make it neater, but it's fine to just serve it from the tin.)

Now move on to the beef and trimmings. Keep the oven at 200°C/gas mark 6. Place a large frying pan over a high heat and add 1 teaspoon of the oil. Carefully place the beef in the pan and brown on all sides – you want a really good colour, so this will take about 10 minutes. Transfer the meat to a roasting tray and pop in the oven for approximately 20 minutes, depending on how you like your meat cooked; 20 minutes will make it medium rare. Once it's out of the oven, it will need to rest for 15 minutes.

Whilst the beef is cooking, make the shallot purée. Place the shallots in a saucepan with the butter and thyme. Cook over a low to medium heat for about 20 minutes until the shallots are translucent and starting to caramelise, then season and add the cream. Remove from the heat and use a hand blender to blitz to a very fine purée. Set aside in the saucepan so that you can give it a quick reheat before you serve.

Wipe the pan that you fried the beef in with kitchen paper and add another teaspoon of oil. Heat it up until it's as hot as possible. Now cut the onions in half and remove the skin, but try not to trim too much off the top and bottom, as you want to keep the beautiful shape of the onion. Place the onions flat-side down in the pan and cook until the flat side is completely charred and black, which will take about 8–10 minutes. Take off the heat, and about 5 minutes before you are ready to eat, place them in the oven to warm through.

When you are ready to go, cook the mushrooms. Place a frying pan over a high heat and add the final teaspoon of olive oil, then the mushrooms. Quickly fry for 5 minutes, getting them golden brown, then add the garlic and parsley. Season with salt and pepper and cook for another 5 minutes. Meanwhile, place the shallot purée back on the heat to warm through.

When you're ready to serve, place a dollop of shallot purée on each plate, followed by a wedge of gratin, a few slices of beef and the mushrooms. Separate the onions into layers to make beautiful petal shapes (see picture). Totally gorgeous!!

Chargrilled hanger steak with cucumber pickle and gochujang hollandaise

★★★ *Hanger steak is a great cut with a really good flavour, but it's a strong, muscly piece and can be tough. Don't overcook it, and when you slice it, slice it against the grain, as this shortens the fibres and makes it more tender. You can't beat a bit of hollandaise with a steak, but I like to add a touch of spice to cut through the richness. Gochujang is a Korean chilli paste – yes, it's a bit trendy, but it does taste good and is worth experimenting with.*

2094 ENERGY KJ	505 ENERGY KCAL	35g PROTEIN	39.8g FAT	22.9g SATURATED FAT	0.7g CARBOHYDRATES	0.7g TOTAL SUGARS	0.1g FIBRE	2.1g SALT

SERVES 4

4 x 150g hanger steaks
sea salt and freshly ground
** black pepper**

For the cucumber pickle
1 cucumber, peeled, cut in half
** lengthways, seeds scooped out**
** and finely sliced on the diagonal**
1 teaspoon salt
200ml white wine vinegar
50g stevia

For the hollandaise sauce
2 free-range egg yolks
1 teaspoon Vinegar and Shallot
** Reduction (see below right)**
150g clarified butter, slightly warmed
1 tablespoon gochujang paste
squeeze of lemon juice

First, make the cucumber pickle. Place the cucumber slices in a bowl. Rub the salt in and leave for 15 minutes.

Mix the vinegar and stevia together in a small saucepan over a medium heat. Bring to the boil and then simmer for 5 minutes. Take off the heat and leave to cool, then pour over the cucumber.

To make the hollandaise, place the egg yolks and Vinegar and Shallot Reduction in a bowl over a saucepan of boiling water. Whisk together until light and fluffy. Slowly add the butter, whisking as you go, to make a thick and glossy sauce. Now add the gochujang, some salt and lots of black pepper, and finally a squeeze of lemon. Set aside in a warmish place, but not hot, as it will split.

Place a frying pan over a high heat until really hot. Season the steaks heavily, then add to the pan and cook for about 4 minutes on each side, depending on how you like your steak cooked. Remove from the heat and let the meat rest for 5 minutes, then carve the steaks against the grain and serve with the pickle and hollandaise.

Vinegar and shallot reduction

Simply place **2 shallots, finely diced, ½ teaspoon black peppercorns, a sprig of thyme** and **400ml white wine vinegar** in a small saucepan, bring to the boil and then simmer until reduced by half. This will keep in the fridge for a few weeks.

Spring lamb, pea and broad bean casserole

★★☆ *One complaint I have when following a high-protein, low-carb eating plan is that it can all seem a bit 'cold' and lacking in comfort. I definitely don't want to live on a diet of nothing but grilled meats and salads – I need some heart-warming stews and casseroles, too. Lamb neck is my favourite cut to use for stews; it's got great flavour, it's not too expensive and it melts in the mouth when cooked just right. A lot of people associate casseroles with winter, but I've made this a springtime version – the mint and peas brighten it all up.*

2290 ENERGY KJ	550 ENERGY KCAL	46.8g PROTEIN	30.9g FAT	12.7 SATURATED FAT	18g CARBOHYDRATES	7.7g TOTAL SUGARS	10g FIBRE	1.8g SALT

SERVES 4

1 tablespoon olive oil

750g lamb neck fillet, cubed

2 celery sticks, chopped

2 garlic cloves, finely sliced

2 leeks, sliced

4 shallots, halved

1 litre vegetable stock

100ml white wine

200g frozen peas

200g frozen broad beans, defrosted
and peeled

a bunch of asparagus spears,
trimmed

a small handful of freshly chopped
flat-leaf parsley

a small handful of freshly chopped
mint, plus extra leaves to garnish

salt and freshly ground black pepper

Place a frying pan over a high heat until smoking hot. Add the oil, followed by the lamb. Sear on all sides and cook until golden brown, seasoning as you go along. After about 10 minutes, when the lamb is browned, add the celery, garlic, leeks and shallots. Continue frying over a medium heat for a further 10 minutes until everything is slightly golden and translucent.

Add the stock and wine and bring to the boil. When it reaches boiling point, reduce the heat to a simmer and skim off any froth or scum. Keep on a low simmer for 1½ to 2 hours – until the meat is tender. Add the peas, broad beans and asparagus, then the parsley and mint, and cook for 5 more minutes.

Check the seasoning and serve, garnished with extra mint leaves if you wish.

Oysters grilled with lardo

★★☆ *I've only enjoyed grilled oysters more recently, and they definitely have their place in this plan. Seafood is one of my favourite ingredients, and oysters are low in fat and high in zinc – plus they are SEXY! They make you feel great, which I think good food should do. A touch of garlic butter and creamy, melting lardo works a treat. You can get lardo from a good deli and most supermarkets. It is essentially cured FAT(!), but a little goes a long way – and it tastes damn good.*

1467 ENERGY KJ	354 ENERGY KCAL	20.3g PROTEIN	28.5g FAT	15.6g SATURATED FAT	4.3g CARBOHYDRATES	0.4g TOTAL SUGARS	0.5g FIBRE	3.5g SALT

SERVES 4 as a starter, or 2 as a main with salad

12 slices lardo (or fatty pancetta), cut very finely

12 rock oysters, live, heavy and closed

lemon wedges, to serve

For the garlic butter (this makes about 10 portions, so keep the rest in the freezer)

250g butter

3 garlic cloves, finely chopped

1 tablespoon freshly chopped flat-leaf parsley

First, make the garlic butter. Soften the butter by bringing it up to room temperature (you can use a microwave if you wish), then mix together with the garlic and parsley. Lay a sheet of clingfilm on the work surface, then spoon the butter in a line down the middle. Shape into a sausage shape and then roll up and wrap tightly. I keep this in the freezer to slice and use whenever I need it.

When you are ready to cook, preheat a grill to its highest setting and open the oysters (see Tip below). Add about ½ teaspoon of the garlic butter and a slice of lardo to each oyster. Pop under the grill and cook for about 4 minutes. Serve hot with lemon wedges.

Chef's tip: *To open oysters, place a chopping board securely on the work surface, then wrap a tea towel over one hand and use it to hold the oyster firmly at the opening, larger end (not where the hinge is). Using an oyster shucking knife in the other hand, place the tip of the shucking knife at the base of the hinge, twist the knife (using some pressure), then, without pressure, lever the knife upwards or twist it to prise open the hinge. Slide the knife under the top shell to release the oyster and open the shell.*

Baked spiced jalapeño crab

★★★ *I had a baked crab dish on the menu when I first opened Pont St that was very popular with customers. I had just returned from filming in the US, and flavours like Old Bay Spice were getting into my cooking (check it out, it's a brilliant spice mix for seafood). Then, years later, I developed this recipe further for a Channel 4 show about helping people relate to their food more. It's a rich dish and I would suggest making it to share. It's pretty sexy, and feels wonderfully indulgent. It is higher in calories than most of my dishes, so just make sure you don't have it EVERY meal time.*

3269 ENERGY KJ	790 ENERGY KCAL	38.1g PROTEIN	68.8g FAT	40.4g SATURATED FAT	5.9g CARBOHYDRATES	2.9g TOTAL SUGARS	2.5g FIBRE	1.5g SALT

SERVES 2

50g butter

2 spring onions, sliced

1 red chilli, diced

1 garlic clove, diced

½ teaspoon celery salt

½ teaspoon smoked paprika

½ teaspoon dried oregano

250g white crabmeat

125g brown crabmeat

zest of 1 lemon

1 tablespoon freshly chopped
   flat-leaf parsley

chicory, celery and carrots, to serve

sea salt and freshly ground black
   pepper

For the jalapeño hollandaise

1 free-range egg yolk

½ teaspoon Vinegar and Shallot
   Reduction (see page 119)

75g clarified butter

squeeze of lemon juice

½ tablespoon chopped jalapeños

dash of Tabasco green jalapeño
   sauce

Heat the butter in a small frying pan over a low heat and gently fry the spring onions, chilli and garlic for about 5 minutes. Then add the celery salt, smoked paprika, oregano and ½ teaspoon black pepper and cook for another minute. Finally, add the crab, lemon zest and parsley. Then season to taste with salt and pepper and spoon into two little dishes or ramekins.

Preheat the oven to 200°C/gas mark 6 or preheat the grill to medium.

To make the hollandaise, place the egg yolk and Vinegar and Shallot Reduction in a metal mixing bowl, then place the mixing bowl over a pan of hot water. Whisk together until light and fluffy, then gradually pour in the clarified butter, whisking all the time. Do not add too much in one go, as the mixture will split. When all the butter is added, season, then squeeze in some lemon juice and add the jalapeños and hot sauce.

Spoon the hollandaise on top of the crab mixture and bake or grill for 4 minutes. Serve with chicory leaves, celery and carrot sticks for dipping into the hot crab.

Saffron and tomato braised mussels and clams with clementine gremolata

★★☆ *Mussels and clams are an excellent source of protein. I have done them here with a punchy tomato sauce that can be eaten with a spoon afterwards. The gremolata is my take on the classic; I've used clementine instead of lemon, which really lifts the dish and takes it to the next level.*

1242 ENERGY KJ	298 ENERGY KCAL	22.3g PROTEIN	15.9g FAT	2.3g SATURATED FAT	12.1g CARBOHYDRATES	6.3g TOTAL SUGARS	2.8g FIBRE	0.7g SALT

SERVES 4

50ml extra virgin olive oil

2 banana shallots, sliced

3 garlic cloves, sliced

a pinch of dried chilli flakes

a large pinch of saffron threads

splash of Pernod

50ml white wine

1 x 400g can chopped tomatoes

1 litre fish stock

300g live mussels, scrubbed and
    debearded

300g live clams, scrubbed

salt and freshly ground black pepper

For the clementine and parsley gremolata

a handful of freshly chopped flat-leaf
    parsley

a handful of freshly chopped
    tarragon

zest of 2 clementines

1 garlic clove, finely chopped

Place a large shallow saucepan over a medium heat and add the olive oil. Then add the shallots, garlic and chilli flakes. Cook for a couple of minutes until the shallots are translucent, then add the saffron, Pernod and white wine. Cook for another 2 minutes, then stir in the tomatoes and stock. Season and simmer, covered, for 20 minutes to let all of the flavours combine. Stir occasionally to stop the mixture sticking.

After 20 minutes, add the mussels and clams and cook for 10 minutes until they are all open (discard any that remain closed).

Meanwhile, make the gremolata by simply mixing all the ingredients together in a bowl.

When you are ready to eat, serve the mussels and clams in a big bowl, with a sprinkling of the gremolata on top.

Lemongrass and turmeric fish cakes

★★☆ *Fish cakes are one of those dishes that fit well into a weekday supper but so often are full of carbs and lacking in taste. I am really into turmeric – I love its scent and flavour. It also contains a lot of antioxidants and anti-inflammatories. Admittedly, you would have to eat a hell of a lot of these fish cakes for the turmeric to truly have an impact, but little by little is still better than nothing! You can leave the crabmeat out of this recipe for a more budget-friendly version, and I like adding sweetcorn to the mix sometimes, too (this is especially good for kids) – although then you are adding carbs, of course, so that would be better for later on in your weight-loss journey.*

872 ENERGY KJ	209 ENERGY KCAL	25.6g PROTEIN	11.4g FAT	4g SATURATED FAT	1.2g CARBOHYDRATES	0.4g TOTAL SUGARS	0.1g FIBRE	1.1g SALT

SERVES 4

200g skinless salmon fillet, cut into large chunks

200g skinless haddock fillet, cut into large chunks

100g white crabmeat

1 tablespoon soy sauce

1 free-range egg yolk

1 tablespoon coconut oil

lime wedges and chilli sauce, to serve

For the paste

1 lemongrass stalk

1 spring onion

2.5cm piece of fresh ginger, peeled

1 green chilli

1 tablespoon freshly chopped coriander

1 teaspoon fresh turmeric purée or ground turmeric

1 teaspoon lime zest

Place all the paste ingredients in a food processor and blitz to form a paste. Spoon it into a bowl and set aside.

Place the salmon and haddock in the food processor and blitz to a paste. Add this to the bowl with the other paste.

Add the crab, soy sauce and egg yolk to the fish mixture and mix well. Shape the mixture into eight little patties using your hands.

Heat up the coconut oil in a pan over a medium heat and pan fry the patties for about 5 minutes on each side. You will need to work in batches, so keep the patties warm in a low oven while you cook the remainder. Serve with lime wedges and chilli sauce.

Malay fish curry

★★✶ *A good, coconut-laced, aromatic fish curry is a guaranteed crowd pleaser. If you're trying to lose weight, remember to keep off the rice – once you've reached your optimum weight and just want to maintain it, some cooked wild rice/basmati mix is good. I love this curry with just the coconut sambal, but will often have some roasted butternut squash or steamed pak choi, too.*

877 ENERGY KJ	212 ENERGY KCAL	29.5g PROTEIN	5.1g FAT	3g SATURATED FAT	13.2g CARBOHYDRATES	8.3g TOTAL SUGARS	0.9g FIBRE	2.3g SALT

SERVES 4

1 teaspoon coconut oil

3 shallots, sliced

1 red chilli, sliced

400ml coconut milk

75ml fish sauce

1 teaspoon sugar

1 teaspoon salt

3 kaffir lime leaves

12 live mussels, scrubbed and debearded

300g monkfish, prepped and cut into large cubes

150g squid rings

8 raw king prawns, shelled and deveined

a handful of freshly chopped coriander

For the paste (makes enough for two curries)

1 tablespoon coconut oil

4 garlic cloves, peeled

4 shallots, peeled

10cm piece of fresh ginger, peeled

5cm piece of galangal, peeled

4 lemongrass stalks

4 red chillies

1 tablespoon ground turmeric

1 strip of lime zest

Place all the curry paste ingredients in a food processor and blitz to a fine paste. Set aside. It will keep in the fridge for 7–10 days.

Place a large, deep saucepan over a medium heat. Add the coconut oil and fry the shallots off until translucent. Add the chilli and half of the curry paste (save the rest for the next curry) and cook for 5 minutes, stirring all the time.

Add the coconut milk, fish sauce, sugar, salt and lime leaves and cook for 10 minutes. Then add the mussels, monkfish and squid. Cook for a further 5 minutes before adding the prawns and coriander. Cook for 4 more minutes until the prawns are pink, then serve with Coconut Sambal (see below) and a wedge of lime.

Coconut sambal

In a bowl, mix together **1 fresh coconut, thin brown 'skin' on, grated, 2 shallots, finely diced, 2 red chillies, finely diced, 1 teaspoon fish sauce** and the **juice of 1 lime**. Season with **sea salt and freshly ground black pepper** and serve.

558 ENERGY KJ	135 ENERGY KCAL	1.6g PROTEIN	13.6g FAT	11.8g SATURATED FAT		
2g CARBOHYDRATES	2g TOTAL SUGARS	2.9g FIBRE	0.5g SALT			

Pan-fried lemon sole fillets with samphire and bottarga butter

★★☆ *This is one of my signature dishes from Pont St. Bottarga is dried mullet roe from Sardinia. I spent a lot of time in Sardinia a few years ago and the food is amazing. Bottarga is traditionally used grated on pasta, but as you'll see throughout this book, I serve it with burrata, on veggies and with fish. It's quite addictive and quite easy to get hold of now – it can be found in Italian delicatessens or online.*

SERVES 4

1 teaspoon olive oil

4 lemon sole fillets (about 150g each)

300g trimmed samphire

squeeze of lemon juice

salt and freshly ground black pepper

For the bottarga butter

100g bottarga

150g butter, at room temperature

zest of 1 lemon

Begin by making the bottarga butter. Grate three-quarters of the bottarga into a bowl, then add the butter and lemon zest. Mix well to fully combine. Lay a sheet of clingfilm on the work surface, then spoon the butter in a line down the middle. Shape into a sausage shape and then roll up and wrap tightly. I keep this in the freezer to slice and use whenever I need it.

When you are ready to eat, heat up a large frying pan over a medium heat and then add a touch of oil. Season the sole fillets and pan-fry for about 3 minutes on each side. Then remove from the pan and keep warm in a low oven.

Add the samphire to the same pan you cooked the fish in, along with four slices of the bottarga butter – the slices should be very fine, and you should use up about half of the butter. Cook for about 5 minutes, then add a squeeze of lemon juice.

Take out four plates and place a sole fillet on each one. Top with the samphire and spoon over the remaining butter and juices in the pan. Slice the remaining bottarga and scatter on top, then serve!

Pan-seared mackerel with radish, apple and watercress salad and salsa verde

★★☆ *This is a fresh, summery dish that is packed full of goodness. Mackerel is a great budget-friendly fish and is full of omega-3s. Salsa verde literally translates as 'green sauce', and there are a million different versions of it, so this is mine. I think it is better cut by hand. It's my go-to sauce and I serve it with fish, grilled lamb chops and poached chicken. This dish is a prime example of why calorie counting alone doesn't work. The calories may look high, but the meal is full of nutrients and healthy fats, so really is good for you.*

3338 ENERGY KJ	804 ENERGY KCAL	58.5g PROTEIN	61.7g FAT	11.8g SATURATED FAT	4.8g CARBOHYDRATES	2.7g TOTAL SUGARS	1.2g FIBRE	1.3g SALT

SERVES 4

8 fresh mackerel fillets (about 150g each)

1 green apple, cored and cut into julienne strips

8 radishes, finely sliced

1 bunch of watercress, stalks picked and discarded

salt and freshly ground black pepper

For the salsa verde

a bunch of fresh basil

a bunch of fresh tarragon

a bunch of fresh mint

½ bunch of fresh flat-leaf parsley

2 garlic cloves, peeled

4 anchovy fillets

100g capers

juice of 2 lemons

50ml extra virgin olive oil

I like to hand cut all the salsa verde ingredients, but you can do it on the pulse setting in a food processor if you prefer. Finely chop all the ingredients and mix together in a bowl. Set aside so that all the flavours can marinate together.

When you are ready to go, place a small frying pan over a high heat until very hot. Lightly season the mackerel fillets and then flash fry for a couple of minutes on each side.

Arrange the apple, radishes and watercress on four plates, then top each with a couple of mackerel fillets and a good dollop of the salsa verde.

Cod with braised fennel and cockle dressing

✳✳✳ *Fennel is a really versatile vegetable. Here I have braised it with saffron, orange and sweet wine, but I also use it in salads, roasts, soups... the list goes on. I used some gorgeous British cockles for the dressing, but if you can't get them, just make the dressing without and this becomes a super-simple meal. You can use any white fish for this dish – I vary it with sea bass, hake or halibut when I am feeling flush.*

1851 ENERGY KJ	444 ENERGY KCAL	38g PROTEIN	26.8g FAT	3.9g SATURATED FAT	6.5g CARBOHYDRATES	6.3g TOTAL SUGARS	2.4g FIBRE	2g SALT

SERVES 4

4 thick-cut pieces of cod fillet (about 150g each)

salt and freshly ground black pepper

For the braised fennel

1 teaspoon olive oil

2 fennel bulbs, finely sliced

2 banana shallots, finely sliced

100ml sweet dessert wine

generous pinch of saffron threads

50ml orange juice

For the cockle dressing

300g live cockles, washed

50ml white wine

100ml extra virgin olive oil

juice of 2 lemons

a handful of freshly chopped tarragon

100g cherry tomatoes

Begin by cooking the fennel. Place a deep frying pan over a medium heat. Add the olive oil, fennel and shallots and sweat down for about 10 minutes, making sure not to colour. Then add the sweet wine, saffron and the orange juice, season and cook until golden and softened – this should take about 30 minutes.

Now move on to the cockle dressing. Heat a saucepan over a high heat and chuck in the cockles and the wine. Cover with a lid and cook until the shells are open – this should take about 4 minutes. Discard any shells that have remained closed. Remove from the heat and let cool. Strain the cooking liquid and set aside.

When cool enough to handle, remove the flesh from the cockle shells and set aside. Mix the cooking liquid with the olive oil, lemon juice and chopped tarragon. Then quarter the tomatoes and add, along with the cockle meat.

To cook the cod, heat up a frying pan over a medium heat. Season the cod well and place in the frying pan, skin-side down. Cook for 8 minutes on this side until the skin is deep golden brown and crisp, then flip over and cook on the other side for 4 minutes until cooked through. Reheat the fennel and then plate up with the cod on top and a couple of spoonfuls of the cockle dressing. Any leftover dressing will keep for about 2 days in the fridge.

Chargrilled prawns with ouzo butter

★★★ *You really can't beat sweet barbecued prawns with garlic butter... unless you add the stunning aniseed vibes of ouzo to the mix. This is inspired by my summers spent in Greece with my family, where a similar dish, Shrimp Saganaki, is very popular. I love involved meals like this – I adore sitting there fiddling with the tasty prawns, chatting over some good white wine and invariably getting myself covered in butter. Really, the perfect lunch.*

1423 ENERGY KJ	345 ENERGY KCAL	7.2g PROTEIN	31.1g FAT	19.6g SATURATED FAT	4.9g CARBOHYDRATES	4.5g TOTAL SUGARS	0.5g FIBRE	1.3g SALT

SERVES 4
16 raw large, shell-on king prawns
salt and freshly ground black pepper

For the ouzo butter
50ml ouzo (or Pernod)
150g butter
2 garlic cloves, finely chopped
a small handful of freshly chopped
    flat-leaf parsley
juice of ½ lemon, plus 2 extra
    lemons, halved, to serve

Clean the prawns and shell them, but keep the heads and tails on. Score down the middle of the back with a sharp knife, and remove the black vein.

Mix together all the ouzo butter ingredients in a small saucepan and bring to the boil. Simmer for a couple of minutes to cook the garlic gently, then remove from the heat.

Heat up a griddle pan over a high heat. Season the prawns and grill for about 3 minutes on each side until charred and cooked through.

Divide the prawns between four plates and pour over the butter. Serve with the extra lemon, along with some herby green salad.

Rainbow trout with little gem, peas, mint and tarragon

✱✱✱ *Trout is a wonderful fish that feels a bit old school and ignored. In fact, it has a beautiful and delicate flavour, plus it's easy to find and budget friendly. I have used rainbow trout here. Aesthetically the pinks and greens are very pleasing, but the dish also feels clean and fresh to eat. Sea trout is another favourite of mine and would also work well with these flavours.*

1593 ENERGY KJ	381 ENERGY KCAL	35.8g PROTEIN	21.9g FAT	8.8g SATURATED FAT	10.9g CARBOHYDRATES	3.9g TOTAL SUGARS	5.5g FIBRE	1.7g SALT

SERVES 4

50g butter

4 spring onions, trimmed but
    left whole

2 little gem lettuces, trimmed
    and halved

400g frozen peas

50ml vegetable stock

4 rainbow trout fillets (about
    150g each)

a handful of fresh mint, roughly torn

a handful of fresh tarragon, roughly
    torn

1 tablespoon olive oil

salt and freshly ground black pepper

lemon wedges, to serve

Heat up a deep frying pan or sauté pan over a medium heat. Add the butter, then the spring onions. Take the little gem lettuce halves and nestle them into the pan, flat-side down. Then add the peas and the stock. Bring to the boil and season, then simmer for 10 minutes.

Meanwhile, cook the sea trout. Heat a frying pan over a medium heat. Season the skin of the fish and place it in the pan, skin-side down. Cook for about 8 minutes on this side until you have a lovely golden crust. Then flip it over and finish off for a few minutes – keep it deep pink inside to make sure it's still moist.

Scatter the mint and tarragon into the peas and lettuce mixture, then drizzle with the olive oil. Serve with the sea trout and a wedge of lemon.

Coconut prawns with green papaya, chilli and coriander salad

✳✳✳ *Yes, I am a bit mad about coconuts. My love of coconut started when I first went to Bali as a child; now it's super fashionable and I am still as loyal as ever. This is my way of having some crunchy deep-fried action with fewer carbs. I had something similar in Miami and it's a really colourful, sunshine-drenched dish... even if you are in the rainy old UK!*

2073 ENERGY KJ	501 ENERGY KCAL	14.1g PROTEIN	43.8g FAT	35.7g SATURATED FAT	13.3g CARBOHYDRATES	11.2g TOTAL SUGARS	7g FIBRE	0.8g SALT

SERVES 4

1 tablespoon coconut flour

2 free-range eggs, beaten

100g desiccated coconut

20 large king prawns, shelled and deveined

100g coconut oil

For the salad

1 green papaya, peeled and deseeded

1 carrot

1 large white radish, peeled

1 cucumber

2 spring onions, sliced

For the dressing

1 red chilli, deseeded

1 teaspoon lime juice

a small handful of fresh coriander leaves

1 teaspoon fish sauce

1 teaspoon runny honey

1 tablespoon soy sauce

Begin by making the dressing. Put all the ingredients in a food processor and blitz together, then set aside.

For the salad, I like to use a spiraliser for the papaya, carrot, radish and cucumbers as everything comes out looking the same. If you don't have one, you can just slice everything into strips instead. Then add to a bowl, along with the sliced spring onions. Pour over the dressing, toss and set aside.

Now move on to the prawns. Put the flour in one bowl, the beaten eggs in another and the desiccated coconut in a third. Dip each prawn in the flour, then the egg, and finally the coconut and place on a plate. Repeat with all the prawns.

Now pour the coconut oil into a large, deep frying pan over a medium heat. It will take about 7–8 minutes to reach the right temperature, but be careful not to overheat. Gently fry the prawns, in batches, for 4–6 minutes until golden brown. Then serve with the salad.

Pan-fried halloumi with pomegranate and preserved lemon salsa

★☆☆ Fried, hot cheese is something that gets me every time. Halloumi is a really useful cheese to have in the fridge for quick salads or breakfasts. Here, I have dressed it with a sweet, sour, salty salsa, using Moroccan preserved lemons and pomegranate. It's a beautiful, jewel-like dish that makes a lovely vegetarian main. If you want to add something extra, the Braised Tomato, Olive Oil and Green Beans on page 157 would go really well.

1397 ENERGY KJ	337 ENERGY KCAL	14.4g PROTEIN	28g FAT	12.4g SATURATED FAT	7.1g CARBOHYDRATES	6.3g TOTAL SUGARS	1.5g FIBRE	0+g SALT

SERVES 4

250g halloumi cheese, cut into 1cm slices

50g rocket

For the salsa

4 small preserved lemons

150g pomegranate seeds

50ml olive oil

juice of 1 lemon

1 tablespoon pomegranate molasses

a handful of freshly chopped mint

Begin by making the salsa. Take the preserved lemons and cut them into quarters, then cut out the flesh inside so that you are left with just the rind. Dice this into little squares and transfer to a bowl. Mix in the remaining salsa ingredients and set aside.

Now heat a frying pan over a high heat and add the halloumi slices. Cook for 4–5 minutes on each side until golden brown.

To serve, arrange the rocket leaves on a plate or platter, then top with the halloumi and salsa.

Caponata

★ ★ ★ *Caponata is a Sicilian vegetable stew, not dissimilar to ratatouille. The main difference is that it has a more sweet and sour taste, called* agre dolce *in Italy. Caponata goes with just about everything. I serve it hot with roast lamb and chicken, cold with burrata and Parma ham or just eat it out of a bowl on its own.*

1415 ENERGY KJ	343 ENERGY KCAL	3.3g PROTEIN	34.2g FAT	4.3g SATURATED FAT	6g CARBOHYDRATES	4.8g TOTAL SUGARS	2.2g FIBRE	0.8g SALT

SERVES 4

100ml olive oil

4 celery sticks, cut into 1cm dice

1 red onion, cut into 1cm dice

1 red pepper, cut into 1cm dice

1 aubergine, cut into 1cm dice

200g canned chopped tomatoes

50g capers

50ml balsamic vinegar

50g pine nuts, toasted

1 small bunch of basil leaves, torn

sea salt and freshly ground
    black pepper

Heat half of the olive oil in a large frying pan. Add the celery, onion and red pepper and fry for a few minutes.

In a separate frying pan, heat the remaining oil over a very high heat and quickly fry the aubergine off. Now add the aubergine to the other pan with the celery, onion and pepper. Stir in the canned tomatoes and capers and simmer for 20 minutes, or until starting to thicken.

Season and add the balsamic vinegar and pine nuts. Finally, add the basil and then either serve hot or leave to cool and serve cold.

Roasted carrot, pickled beets and labneh salad with truffle honey and pistachios

✷✷✷ *I developed this dish as a vegetarian option for the Royal polo match I cater for every year. Princes William and Harry both play at the match and it is such a lovely event. During the tasting, the charity loved this dish so much that they wanted it for all the guests. It does take some time to plate it – in fact, it took my team 4 hours to plate the 500 dishes. You can take as much time as you want – and you probably won't be serving 500!*

1878 ENERGY KJ	451 ENERGY KCAL	10.9g PROTEIN	27.6g FAT	7.8g SATURATED FAT	36.6g CARBOHYDRATES	35.1g TOTAL SUGARS	5.5g FIBRE	0.9g SALT

SERVES 4

12 baby carrots

1 tablespoon olive oil

1 yellow heirloom carrot

1 orange carrot

1 purple heirloom carrot

drizzle of Classic Dressing (page 68)

300g labneh (or full-fat Greek yogurt)

2 raw baby candy stripe beetroot, finely sliced

handful of pea shoots

100g pistachios, chopped

100g truffle honey

salt and freshly ground black pepper

For the pickled beets (makes enough for about 3 salads/12 servings)

3 bunches of baby yellow beetroot, leaves and stalks trimmed

3 bunches of baby purple beetroot, leaves and stalks trimmed

500ml cider vinegar

200g caster sugar

1 teaspoon black peppercorns

1 teaspoon fennel seeds

1 red chilli, halved lengthways

2 garlic cloves, peeled

Begin by making the pickled beets. Place the yellow beets in one saucepan and the purple in another and cover both with water. Bring to the boil and then simmer for 15–20 minutes until tender. Take off the heat, drain and leave to cool. Once cool, rub the skin off with your hands. Try to keep the stalks attached. Transfer to two bowls, still keeping the colours separate.

Pour the vinegar into a saucepan and add the sugar, peppercorns and fennel seeds. Bring to the boil, then reduce the heat and simmer for 10 minutes. When all the sugar has dissolved, take off the heat and add the chilli and garlic. Now pour half of the vinegar mixture over the yellow beets and half over the purple beets. Transfer to two separate containers, seal and place in the fridge.

Preheat the oven to 200°C/gas mark 6. Place the baby carrots on a roasting tray, drizzle with the olive oil and season with salt and pepper. Roast for 10 minutes until cooked through and golden.

Use the peeler to peel the other carrots into thin strips. Place in a bowl, season and drizzle over a touch of the dressing.

Finally, after all that prep you can plate it! Spread some of the labneh (or yogurt) across each plate and then arrange the pickled and candy beets and roasted and stripped carrots across it. Scatter over the pea shoots and pistachios, drizzle with the truffle honey and serve.

Asparagus with bottarga butter

★★☆ *My favourite ingredient again! Bottarga is dried mullet roe from Sardinia. It's got that sought-after umami flavour and is very versatile. I often used to make an anchovy and lemon butter to serve with veggies, but this has now overtaken to become my favourite. A huge pile of this asparagus when it's in season really is beautiful. The bottarga butter is also lovely with fish, lamb chops, grilled veal escalopes... you name it.*

680 ENERGY KJ	165 ENERGY KCAL	4.3g PROTEIN	16g FAT	9.9g SATURATED FAT	1.1g CARBOHYDRATES	1.1g TOTAL SUGARS	0.8g FIBRE	0.3g SALT

SERVES 4 as a side

12 asparagus spears, trimmed

For the bottarga butter

75g bottarga, grated

150g butter

zest of 1 lemon

For the bottarga butter, place the bottarga in a bowl with the butter and lemon zest and mix well. Lay some clingfilm on the work surface, then spoon the butter in a line down the middle. Roll into a sausage shape, wrap tightly and freeze to firm up before slicing.

When you're ready to eat, cook the asparagus in boiling water for 4 minutes, then drain. Serve on a plate with 5–8 slices of the bottarga butter on top. Any leftover bottarga butter can be wrapped up and kept in the freezer.

Sweet, slow-cooked olive oil, garlic and lemon courgettes

★☆☆ *I love courgettes – they are a really dynamic vegetable. When in season, they have a wonderfully sweet flavour, and I love to slow cook them with masses of olive oil and garlic. This can be a dish in itself, sprinkled with a touch of Parmesan or bottarga. It's also great as a side dish with some roast chicken or fish.*

1019 ENERGY KJ	248 ENERGY KCAL	2.3g PROTEIN	25.4g FAT	3.7g SATURATED FAT	2.6g CARBOHYDRATES	1.8g TOTAL SUGARS	1.5g FIBRE	0.8g SALT

SERVES 4 as a side

100ml olive oil

4 garlic cloves, sliced

6 courgettes, diced

zest of 1 lemon

salt and freshly ground black pepper

Place the olive oil in a frying pan over a medium heat. Add the garlic and cook for 5 minutes until translucent – don't let it colour at all. Add the courgettes and continue cooking for about 30 minutes, stirring occasionally. Then season with salt and pepper and grate over the lemon zest before serving.

Chargrilled broccoli with oyster mayonnaise

✱✱✱ Charring vegetables really brings their flavour out, and the technique is worth experimenting with. The oysters add that amazing seaside flavour to the mayonnaise, making it a more complex, special meal. This oyster mayonnaise also goes well with poached salmon and asparagus.

658 ENERGY KJ	158 ENERGY KCAL	7.4g PROTEIN	12.9g FAT	1.9g SATURATED FAT	3.3g CARBOHYDRATES	2.1g TOTAL SUGARS	3.5g FIBRE	0.4g SALT

SERVES 4 as a side

400g tenderstem or purple sprouting broccoli

lemon wedges, to serve

For the oyster mayonnaise

40g pasteurised egg yolks

splash of white wine vinegar

25ml extra virgin olive oil

75ml vegetable oil

1 teaspoon lemon juice

4 live oysters, shucked, juice reserved

salt and freshly ground black pepper

Place a large saucepan of water on to boil. Once it's boiling, add the broccoli and blanch for 4 minutes, then drain and refresh in cold water. Drain well again and set aside.

Now make the mayonnaise. Place the egg yolks and vinegar in a blender and whizz for a few minutes until light and frothy. With the blender still running, gradually pour the oil in until the mixture is really thick and creamy. Add the lemon juice. Pour the oyster juice into the mayonnaise and stir in. Chop the oyster meat and add that to the mayonnaise, too. Taste for seasoning and adjust if necessary.

When you are ready to eat, heat up a griddle pan over a high heat and chargrill the broccoli for a few minutes on each side. Serve with lemon wedges and about 1 tablespoon of the oyster mayonnaise per person. Any leftover mayonnaise will keep in the fridge for about 3 days.

Tofu, chilli, bonito and cucumber salad

★★☆ *I used to think tofu was the ultimate in hippy fodder. My mum would cook it all the time for us when we were kids, but it's taken me 20-odd years to learn to like it. This dish should turn everything you think you know about tofu on its head: fresh, creamy tofu, with chilli, soy and savoury umami flakes. The whole thing is really pure and wholesome. I have this when I have had enough of meat and dairy and just want a clean plate of food.*

574 ENERGY KJ	137 ENERGY KCAL	13.5g PROTEIN	5g FAT	0.6g SATURATED FAT	14.8g CARBOHYDRATES	7.7g TOTAL SUGARS	0.1g FIBRE	2.4g SALT

SERVES 4

100ml white wine vinegar

50g stevia

1 cucumber

1 teaspoon sea salt

2 tablespoons soy sauce

dash of sesame oil

400g soft tofu

30g packet bonito flakes

chilli oil and sesame seeds
  (optional), to serve

Begin by making the cucumber salad. Heat the vinegar and stevia in a saucepan over a medium heat and bring to the boil. Remove from the heat and leave to cool.

Take the cucumber and cut into four lengthways. Deseed it, then cut into smaller pieces and place in a bowl. Add the salt, rub it in and then leave for 15 minutes.

Rinse the salt off and place the cucumber in a clean bowl. Pour over the vinegar mixture and stir to combine, then add the soy sauce and sesame oil and mix well.

Gently slice the tofu and divide between four plates. Add some cucumber salad to the side of each plate, and sprinkle the bonito flakes on top. Drizzle with chilli oil and sprinkle over some sesame seeds (if using), then serve.

Globe artichoke with roasted garlic aioli

★★☆ *Earlier this year I was in Northern California. I find the food scene there really inspiring – they have such amazing produce and I love the simplicity of how things are put together. We drove from San Francisco to Big Sur, and en route passed by field after field of produce, including thousands of artichokes, one of their main ingredients. A perfectly cooked artichoke served warm with some homemade sweet roasted garlic aioli is perfection to me.*

1195 ENERGY KJ	289 ENERGY KCAL	5.5g PROTEIN	28.3g FAT	4.6g SATURATED FAT	4.9g CARBOHYDRATES	1.6g TOTAL SUGARS	0.7g FIBRE	0.8g SALT

SERVES 4

4 large globe artichokes,
    stalks trimmed
juice of 2 lemons

For the aioli
1 garlic bulb
40g pasteurised egg yolks
1 teaspoon Dijon mustard
100ml extra virgin olive oil
1 teaspoon lemon juice
salt and freshly ground black pepper

Begin by roasting the garlic for the aioli. Preheat the oven to 200°C/ gas mark 6. Wrap the garlic bulb in foil and roast for 30 minutes until soft. Leave to cool.

Place the artichokes in a large pan of water and squeeze in the lemon juice. Cut a piece of baking paper into a circle and place on top – this will keep the artichokes under water. Bring to the boil, then reduce the heat and simmer for about 45 minutes.

Whilst the artichokes are cooking, you can make the aioli. Squeeze out the roasted garlic cloves into a blender and add the egg yolks and mustard. Blitz until smooth and then, with the blender still running, very slowly pour in the oil until it is all incorporated and a thick, pale sauce has developed. Check the seasoning and add the lemon juice.

To serve, drain off the artichokes and serve whole on a plate with a little bowl of aioli.

As I have said before, I love dishes that you can really get stuck into – the meal takes longer, you can enjoy it more and it feels like you are eating masses, when in fact you are just eating more slowly. With artichokes, you take one leaf off at a time, and strip the meat off with your mouth. When you get to the base, cut off the hairy bit and you will be left with the heart, which you can dip and enjoy – the little prize at the end of it all.

Butternut squash with za'atar

✶✶ Za'atar is a Middle Eastern spice mix. It's found all over the region, and every area has its own variation. It usually contains dried thyme, sumac, sesame seeds and salt. It's great sprinkled on roasted meats, breads, veggies and mixed into olive oil for a dip. I even use it to season popcorn. In Lebanon they flavour croissants with it, which always amuses me as it seems a strange combo. I use it with squash here because it works well with the sweetness. Serve with some little lamb chops or grilled chicken, plus the braised green beans on page 157, and you have a lovely meal.

221 ENERGY KJ	52 ENERGY KCAL	1.4g PROTEIN	0.9g FAT	0.1g SATURATED FAT	10.4g CARBOHYDRATES	5.6g TOTAL SUGARS	2g FIBRE	0.8g SALT

SERVES 4

500g butternut squash, peeled, deseeded and cut into wedges

1 teaspoon olive oil

1 tablespoon za'atar

salt and freshly ground black pepper

Preheat the oven to 200°C/gas mark 6.

Arrange the butternut squash wedges on a roasting tray. Drizzle with the olive oil and season with salt and pepper. Roast for 30–40 minutes until golden brown, then sprinkle with the za'atar and serve.

Celeriac mash

✶✶ Celeriac has a really great, deep, savoury flavour and works well as a potato alternative. Celeriac mash is an old favourite of mine, and I also replace potatoes with celeriac in gratins (see page 116). This mash is great with my Roasted Chicken Thighs with Artichokes and Chorizo (see page 100), or my Spring Lamb Casserole (see page 120).

160 ENERGY KJ	39 ENERGY KCAL	1g PROTEIN	2.1g FAT	0.7g SATURATED FAT	3.2g CARBOHYDRATES	2.5g TOTAL SUGARS	4.7g FIBRE	1.1g SALT

SERVES 4

500g celeriac, peeled and diced

1 tablespoon garlic and herb cream cheese, such as Boursin

1 teaspoon butter

salt and freshly ground black pepper

Place the celeriac in a saucepan and cover with water. Bring to the boil and then simmer for 30 minutes.

Drain, then return to the pan along with the cream cheese and butter. Season with salt and pepper and then blitz with a hand blender to your desired texture. Reheat before serving.

Miso-glazed charred cabbage

★★☆ *I first tried miso when I was a young child. My mother used to make us miso soup with nori seaweed as a very healthy supper. I can't remember exactly my thoughts at that age, but I know I have always loved its umami richness. I use miso more in glazes, marinades and dressings now than anything, and it really works with veggies. This particular glaze is also great with Brussels sprouts.*

162 ENERGY KJ	39 ENERGY KCAL	1.5g PROTEIN	1.1g FAT	0.1g SATURATED FAT	5.8g CARBOHYDRATES	4.8g TOTAL SUGARS	1.2g FIBRE	1.7g SALT

SERVES 4 as a side

2 tablespoons tamari

1 teaspoon sesame oil

1 tablespoon miso

1 tablespoon runny honey

1 sweetheart cabbage

sprinkling of shichimi togarashi
   (**Japanese spice mix – if you
   can't get this, you can use chilli
   powder instead**)

freshly ground black pepper

In a bowl, mix together the tamari, sesame oil, miso and honey. Season with black pepper, then add to a small saucepan. Bring to the boil and whisk until well combined.

Take the cabbage and cut it in half down the middle. Place in a saucepan of boiling water over a high heat and blanch for 3 minutes, then drain and refresh under the cold tap. Drain off and dry.

Preheat the grill to very high.

Place the cabbage cut-side up on a baking tray and brush with the miso glaze. Grill for about 8 minutes until the cabbage is charred and black around the edges. Turn over for the last couple of minutes.

Sprinkle with the spice mix and serve.

Roasted spiced cauliflower with paneer

✱✱✱ This is a great vegetarian main course, but will also work as a side dish for grilled meat or curry. Cauliflower tastes great when roasted, as its nutty flavour is revealed, and the paneer provides the protein. You can experiment with the spices to come up with your own perfect blend. To make this a main meal, serve with some lightly spiced spinach and Greek yogurt with mint on the side.

953 ENERGY KJ	229 ENERGY KCAL	18g PROTEIN	17g FAT	10.2g SATURATED FAT	4.2g CARBOHYDRATES	3.4g TOTAL SUGARS	2.3g FIBRE	0.1g SALT

SERVES 4 as a side, 2 as a main

**1 cauliflower, broken into evenly
    sized small florets**
230g paneer
2 limes, cut into wedges
fresh coriander leaves, to serve

For the spice mix
splash of vegetable oil
1 teaspoon ground cumin
1 teaspoon ground coriander
1 teaspoon ground turmeric
pinch of chilli powder
1 teaspoon yellow mustard seeds
2 cardamom pods, crushed

Preheat the oven to 200°C/gas mark 6.

Place the spice mix ingredients in a bowl and mix together thoroughly. Add the cauliflower florets and paneer and mix everything together so that it is coated in the spice mix.

Spread the cauliflower and paneer out on a shallow roasting tray and roast in the oven for 15 minutes. Give it a good shake to turn everything over and return to the oven for another 15 minutes.

Serve with the lime wedges and some coriander leaves.

Braised spring vegetables

★★☆ *For years, vegetables really took a back seat in the UK, unlike in so many countries where they make up the bulk of the cuisine. Happily, these days we are starting to really tap into this positive way to eat. I eat a high-protein diet, but I also eat a huge amount of veggies – they're where I get my carbs and a lot of my nutrients. I could never do the Atkins diet, because it restricts so much fruit and veg, but I can happily live on dishes like this. You can easily adapt this recipe depending on what's in season, but this is my favourite combo – it's so colourful and vibrant.*

484 ENERGY KJ	117 ENERGY KCAL	1.4g PROTEIN	10.6g FAT	6.6g SATURATED FAT	4.6g CARBOHYDRATES	2.1g TOTAL SUGARS	1.4g FIBRE	1g SALT

SERVES 4

4 baby carrots, trimmed

4 baby courgettes, trimmed and
    halved lengthways

4 patty pans, halved

8 breakfast radishes

4 asparagus spears, trimmed

50g butter

a handful of peas

4 prepped and cooked baby
    artichokes (use jarred or canned,
    if you like)

a small handful of chopped tarragon

sea salt and freshly ground black
    pepper

Begin by blanching the vegetables. They all require different times, so you'll need to add them to the water at different points. The carrots need 6 minutes, the courgettes and patty pans need 4 minutes and the radishes and asparagus spears need just 3 minutes.

Once you've blanched the vegetables, refresh them all in cold water and drain.

When you are ready to go, heat the butter up in a deep frying pan over a medium heat. When it has melted, add a splash of water and some salt and pepper, then chuck in all the vegetables (including the peas and artichokes) and the tarragon. Cook for a couple of minutes, stirring, and then serve.

These veggies are a dream with lamb chops, chicken or fish.

Boureki

★★☆ *Boureki is a traditional Greek dish. Some people add a layer of pastry, and it often has a layer of potatoes. I have stuck to the low-carb roots here and kept out both. It really can be a meal in itself, and the mint, ricotta and tomato layers are fresh and comforting at the same time. In Greece it is made with Mizithra (a light cream cheese), but ricotta is similar.*

832 ENERGY KJ	201 ENERGY KCAL	10.1g PROTEIN	16.4g FAT	6.2g SATURATED FAT	3.3g CARBOHYDRATES	2.7g TOTAL SUGARS	0.8g FIBRE	0.4g SALT

SERVES 6

6 courgettes, finely sliced
200g canned tomatoes
150g ricotta
a handful of fresh mint, chopped
1 teaspoon dried oregano
50ml olive oil
100g Parmesan cheese, grated
salt and freshly ground black pepper

Preheat the oven to 180°C/gas mark 4.

In a deep baking dish measuring about 20 x 30cm, start layering up the vegetables. Begin with a layer of courgettes, then tomatoes, then a scattering of ricotta, then mint and oregano. Season each layer and drizzle with a touch of olive oil. Repeat to use up all the vegetables.

Finish the top layer with the Parmesan and bake for 40 minutes, or until cooked through and golden.

Braised tomato, olive oil and green beans

★☆☆ *This is another real Greek vegetable dish. It's a wonderful way to cook green beans, especially at the end of summer, when they are thicker. It can be served cold as part of a meze or hot as a side dish. Don't be scared by the quantity of olive oil: we need some good fats in our bodies to keep us feeling full, and the olive oil is essential to the flavour of this dish.*

768 ENERGY KJ	186 ENERGY KCAL	2.3g PROTEIN	17.3g FAT	2.5g SATURATED FAT	5.6g CARBOHYDRATES	4.1g TOTAL SUGARS	3.4g FIBRE	0.5g SALT

SERVES 6

100ml extra virgin olive oil
1 onion, sliced
2 garlic cloves, sliced
500g green beans, trimmed
300g canned chopped tomatoes
1 teaspoon dried oregano
salt and freshly ground black pepper

Place a heavy-bottomed saucepan over a medium heat and warm up the olive oil. Add the onion and garlic and sweat for 10 minutes.

Now add the green beans, tomatoes, 300ml water and oregano. Season with salt and pepper. Bring to the boil, then reduce the heat and simmer for 40–60 minutes.

So hopefully by now I have established that sugar is not what we want in our diet! For years the government bodies around the world have told us that we should have a high-carb (a.k.a. high-sugar) and low-fat diet, and that has lead to widespread obesity and diabetes. We are starting to realise that sugar is the worst thing for us and that reducing sugar can lead to weight loss and better health. I would happily cut out the desserts in this book, as ideally I would like to encourge you to not eat desserts. But I know that now and again people want them, so I have included a small selection of reduced-sugar sweet treats. Do proceed with caution – these are not for everyday consumption, and if you really want to lose weight and retrain your sugar receptors, you need to try and cut out everything that tastes sweet for the first month of this diet.

Desserts and Little Extras

Dark chocolate truffles

✱✱✱ *I don't eat desserts when I am dieting, but I do crave chocolate now and again, so these are a good little fix. Don't forget the salt! It highlights the chocolate perfectly.*

525 ENERGY KJ	126 ENERGY KCAL	1.3g PROTEIN	9.1g FAT	6.9g SATURATED FAT	10.1g CARBOHYDRATES	9.6g TOTAL SUGARS	0.2g FIBRE	0.1g SALT

MAKES ABOUT 30

250ml double cream

½ teaspoon vanilla extract

pinch of sea salt

500g dark chocolate (about 60% cocoa solids is good), finely chopped

50g cocoa powder

Line two baking sheets with greaseproof paper. Place the cream, vanilla and sea salt in a saucepan over a medium heat. Bring to the boil for a minute, then remove from the heat and add the chocolate. Stir well until all the chocolate has melted, then set aside to cool at room temperature for about 1 hour.

Once cool enough, pour the chocolate mixture into a piping bag and pipe little mounds onto the prepared baking sheets, then place in the fridge for about 1 hour until set. Roll in the cocoa powder and serve. The truffles will keep for a few weeks in the fridge, but bring them to room temperature before eating.

Lemon, coconut and macadamia truffles

✱✱✱ *I was messing around with some sweet ideas and took these along to the book's first photo shoot as a treat for the team. Everyone loved them so much that I had to include them!*

415 ENERGY KJ	101 ENERGY KCAL	1g PROTEIN	10g FAT	4.5g SATURATED FAT	0.9g CARBOHYDRATES	0.9g TOTAL SUGARS	1.4g FIBRE	0.1g SALT

MAKES ABOUT 20

150g macadamia nuts

1 teaspoon vanilla extract

1 teaspoon lemon zest

1 teaspoon lemon juice

2 tablespoons coconut oil

1 teaspoon agave

100g desiccated coconut, for rolling

Line two baking sheets with greaseproof paper. Blitz together the nuts, vanilla extract, lemon zest and juice, coconut oil and agave in a food processor. Transfer the mixture to the fridge and chill for 30 minutes. When it has firmed up a little, take it out and roll up teaspoon-sized amounts into little balls.

Roll in the desiccated coconut to coat. Place the truffles on the prepared baking sheets and chill for at least 1 hour until ready to eat. Serve chilled. These will keep for about 1 week in the fridge.

Peanut and chocolate cups

★★☆ *Peanut butter is extremely popular in my house and we eat it daily (for better or for worse). When my fiancé tried these, he told me he wanted me to open a shop selling nothing but these – apparently they are that amazing! I'm not sure about the shop idea, but I have to say these are seriously good, and a lot better for you than any ready-made variety. It goes without saying that you shouldn't eat too many of these, but keep them in mind for when you need a major treat.*

807 ENERGY KJ	195 ENERGY KCAL	2.8g PROTEIN	16.6g FAT	10.9g SATURATED FAT	9g CARBOHYDRATES	7.9g TOTAL SUGARS	0.6g FIBRE	0.2g SALT

MAKES 24

For the peanut layer

250g peanut butter

100ml maple syrup

100g coconut oil

For the chocolate layer

200g dark chocolate (at least 70 per cent cocoa solids), chopped

100g coconut oil

rock salt, for sprinkling

Take 24 mini foil muffin cases and arrange in a mini muffin tray or on a baking sheet.

Place the peanut butter, maple syrup and coconut oil in a small saucepan and heat over a low heat until combined. Divide the mixture between the cases and chill for 30 minutes to set.

Rinse out the saucepan and add the chocolate and coconut oil. Place over a very low heat and stir until melted together.

Divide this between the cases over the peanut mixture. Sprinkle with a little rock salt and return to the fridge for about 1 hour until set completely.

These will keep in the fridge for 2–3 weeks.

Coconut panna cotta with passion fruit and lime

★★✻ *Panna cottas are one of my favourite desserts: little wobbly mounds of cream and sweetness. I have made a dairy-free version here with coconut cream and milk. They remind me a little of Asian puddings and, as desserts go, they are quite low in sugar. The passion fruit is quite tart and cuts through it all really well, too.*

943 ENERGY KJ	227 ENERGY KCAL	5.2g PROTEIN	17.6g FAT	15.1g SATURATED FAT	9g CARBOHYDRATES	9g TOTAL SUGARS	0.5g FIBRE	0.2g SALT

SERVES 4

4 gelatine leaves

200ml coconut cream

300ml coconut milk

25ml Malibu

2 teaspoons stevia

zest of 1 lime

4 passion fruit, cut into wedges

coconut shavings, to decorate

Place the gelatine leaves in a bowl of cold water to soften.

Pour the coconut cream, coconut milk and Malibu into a saucepan along with the stevia and place over a medium heat. Bring to the boil, then remove from the heat and add the lime zest.

Remove the gelatine from the cold water and squeeze out any excess water. Stir the gelatine into the coconut milk mixture until it dissolves.

Pour the mixture into four metal panna cotta moulds (if you don't have any moulds, you could use ramekins or glasses) and pop into the fridge for a few hours until set.

When you are ready to serve, turn out the panna cottas from the moulds and decorate with the passion fruit and coconut shavings.

Sugar-free vanilla cheesecake with blackberry compote

★★★ *Cheesecake is one of the best desserts ever invented. I have a cheesecake recipe that I love and always go back to. It's a little different to the norm, as it doesn't have a base – it's simply slabs of rich, creamy gorgeousness. I've adapted that recipe to suit this plan a little better, so the recipe below contains less sugar, and I've removed the flour, too. I've added some honey-roasted macadamias for a bit of crunch, so you won't miss that sugary biscuit base.*

2131 ENERGY KJ	517 ENERGY KCAL	5.5g PROTEIN	52.9g FAT	28.3g SATURATED FAT	4.3g CARBOHYDRATES	4.3g TOTAL SUGARS	1.3g FIBRE	0.8g SALT

SERVES 16

1kg cream cheese

100g butter, softened, plus a little
    extra for greasing

4 tablespoons stevia

1 tablespoon vanilla extract

2 tablespoons maple syrup

6 eggs

300ml double cream

zest of 1 lemon, plus 1 teaspoon juice

For the honey-roasted macadamias

200g macadamia nuts

1 tablespoon runny honey

For the blackberry compote

300g blackberries

2 tablespoons stevia

Preheat the oven to 180°C/gas mark 4 and lightly grease a 23cm round cake tin. Line a baking tray with greaseproof paper.

Place the cream cheese, butter, stevia and vanilla extract in a mixing bowl and beat together using an electric or hand whisk. Add the maple syrup and beat well again.

In a separate bowl, whisk the eggs, then gradually add them to the cream cheese mixture. Stir in the cream and lemon zest and juice.

Pour the mixture into the prepared tin. Wrap the outside of the tin in foil and place in a deep roasting tray. Pour water into the roasting tray so that it comes halfway up the side of the cake tin. Place in the oven and cook for 30 minutes, or until just set.

Meanwhile, mix together the nuts and honey in a bowl and spread on the lined baking tray. Roast for 30 minutes until golden and crispy. Remove from the oven, leave to cool and chop roughly.

For the berry compote, place the berries and stevia in a saucepan and bring to the boil. Simmer for 4 minutes, then leave to cool.

When the cheesecake is cooked, take it out of the oven. Leave to cool and chill overnight. Serve a slice of cheesecake with some chopped macadamia nuts and a spoonful of the berry compote.

Pomegranate jellies with mint

✶✶✶ *Jellies make a great low-fat dessert, and I like experimenting with different flavours and juices. This pomegranate and mint one feels quite virtuous. Pomegranate juice is high in antioxidants – just make sure you use a good-quality one, without lots of added sugar.*

523 ENERGY KJ	123 ENERGY KCAL	4.5g PROTEIN	2.7g FAT	1.7g SATURATED FAT	21.7g CARBOHYDRATES	21.5g TOTAL SUGARS	1.7g FIBRE	0.1g SALT

SERVES 4

5 large gelatine leaves

500ml pomegranate juice

200g pomegranate seeds

a small handful of mint leaves to infuse, plus extra to decorate

Greek yogurt, to serve

Place the gelatine leaves in a bowl of cold water to soften.

Pour 200ml of the pomegranate juice into a saucepan and place over a medium heat. Add the mint leaves to infuse. When the juice comes to the boil, simmer for a few minutes, then take off the heat and remove the mint.

Drain the gelatine, squeeze out any excess water and mix it into the hot juice. Transfer the mixture to a jug and stir in the 300ml cold pomegranate juice.

Pour the mixture into four moulds or little glass serving dishes. Place in the fridge for a few hours to set, then serve. If you have used metal moulds, dip them in hot water before turning the jelly out onto a plate, then decorate with pomegranate seeds and extra mint, if you like. Serve with Greek yogurt. If using serving dishes, decorate accordingly and serve.

Ice lollies

✻✻✻ *When you first start on this diet, you'll need to realign your taste buds and avoid all sweet items. I know this can be hard, and for me it was when I started to realise how addicted to sugar we all are! When I really feel in need, I have one of these lollies. They satisfy that craving and make you feel a bit like a big kid – in a good way!*

MAKES 6

These are really just hints for what works, as it depends on the size of your ice-lolly tray. The recipes below are for 70ml lolly moulds, so you might need to vary them slightly according to the size.

Blood orange

98 ENERGY KJ | 23 ENERGY KCAL | 0.4g PROTEIN | 0g FAT | 0g SATURATED FAT | 5.7g CARBOHYDRATES | 5.7g TOTAL SUGARS | 0.1g FIBRE | 0g SALT

Simply pour **420ml blood orange juice** into the lolly moulds, leaving a 5mm gap at the top so that the mixture can expand. Add the lolly sticks and freeze for at least 2 hours. Pink grapefruit juice will also work well for lollies.

Avocado, agave and lime

624 ENERGY KJ | 151 ENERGY KCAL | 1.3g PROTEIN | 13g FAT | 2.7g SATURATED FAT | 7.3g CARBOHYDRATES | 6.6g TOTAL SUGARS | 2.3g FIBRE | 0g SALT

Place **4 avocados, peeled and stoned,** and the **juice of 4 limes** in a blender and blitz until smooth. Add **50g agave syrup** and **150ml water** and mix well. Spoon into the lolly moulds, leaving a 5mm gap at the top so that the mixture can expand. Add the lolly sticks and freeze for at least 2 hours.

Coconut

334 ENERGY KJ | 80 ENERGY KCAL | 0.7g PROTEIN | 5.8g FAT | 4.9g SATURATED FAT | 6.8g CARBOHYDRATES | 6g TOTAL SUGARS | 1.1g FIBRE | 0.2g SALT

Mix together **400ml coconut milk, 50g desiccated coconut** and **25ml coconut syrup**. Pour into the lolly moulds, leaving a 5mm gap at the top so that the mixture can expand. Add the lolly sticks and freeze for at least 2 hours.

Crème brûlée

✳✳✳ *This is a classic dessert that is very simple to make. I have changed it by removing some of the sugar. It still has some, though, as it's needed for the crunchy brûlée topping, so make sure you save this one for special occasions.*

1616 ENERGY KJ	391 ENERGY KCAL	6g PROTEIN	37.1g FAT	22.4g SATURATED FAT	8.2g CARBOHYDRATES	8.2g TOTAL SUGARS	0.1g FIBRE	0.1g SALT

SERVES 6

1 vanilla pod

500ml double cream

3 tablespoons stevia

8 free-range egg yolks

2 tablespoons fruit sugar

Preheat the oven to 160°C/gas mark 3. Split the vanilla pod and scrape out the seeds. Pop the pod and the seeds in a saucepan with the cream and stevia. Place over a medium heat, bring to the boil and then set aside. Remove the vanilla pod.

Whisk the egg yolks in a bowl and then pour in the cream mix.

Take six ramekins and place them in a deep oven dish. Pour water into the dish so that it reaches about halfway up the sides of the ramekins, then divide the mixture between the ramekins.

Carefully place in the oven and cook for 30 minutes, or until just set, but still a bit wobbly. Take out of the oven and leave to cool at room temperature.

Once they've cooled, preheat the grill to high or get a blowtorch ready. Sprinkle the fruit sugar over the top of each ramekin, then either place under the grill for 4–5 minutes, or heat the tops with a blowtorch until deep golden brown. Serve!

Gruyère custard with celery and apple

★★✫ *I am not a big dessert person and will often opt for cheese instead of a sweet, but this is something in between. It is slightly more exciting than a slab of cheese, but still suits a more savoury palate. You can use all sorts of cheese, too: blue cheese would work well, as would an aged Comté. A fragrant piece of poached quince would be gorgeous with this, but you would need to poach it in sugar, so it is not one for this book.*

2065 ENERGY KJ	499 ENERGY KCAL	20.5g PROTEIN	45.7g FAT	27.3g SATURATED FAT	4.4g CARBOHYDRATES	4.4g TOTAL SUGARS	0.5g FIBRE	1.6g SALT

SERVES 4

250ml double cream

1 whole nutmeg, for grating

200g aged Gruyère cheese, grated

4 free-range eggs

2 celery sticks, thinly sliced into
   rounds

1 apple, cored and chopped into
   strips

1 teaspoon Classic Dressing (see
   page 68)

truffle oil, for drizzling

salt and freshly ground black pepper

Preheat the oven to 160°C/gas mark 3.

Place the cream in a saucepan and grate in some nutmeg to taste, then bring to the boil.

Now add the cheese and stir well until it has melted into the cream. Season to taste and remove from the heat.

In a bowl or jug, whisk the eggs together with a pinch of salt, then pour in the cream and cheese mixture and whisk well to combine. Pour the cheese custard into a 12 x 18cm baking dish (choose one that you are happy to serve it from). Place this dish inside a bigger, deep tray, and fill the outer tray with water so that it comes part-way up the sides of the baking dish.

Carefully place in the oven and cook for about 25–35 minutes. You don't want to overcook it, as it will scramble, so keep an eye on it and cook it until wobbly and just set.

While the custard is cooking, prep the celery and apple and dress with the Classic Dressing. When you're ready to eat, serve a big scoop of the cheese custard with the dressed celery and apple, and drizzle with truffle oil.

Hazelnut and dark chocolate cake

★★☆ *My mother is a great cook and she was always a big inspiration for me. When we were growing up, she didn't make many cakes and that was partly down to not wanting to give us too much sugar. She did make a killer hazelnut cake, though, and I have recreated it here. It uses stevia instead of sugar, and doesn't contain any flour, yet it is incredibly good.*

1633 ENERGY KJ	394 ENERGY KCAL	7.3g PROTEIN	33.5g FAT	14.2g SATURATED FAT	16.9g CARBOHYDRATES	15.9g TOTAL SUGARS	1.7g FIBRE	0.2g SALT

SERVES 12

butter or vegetable oil, for greasing

300g hazelnuts

4 tablespoons stevia

8 free-range egg whites

For the chocolate cream

300g dark chocolate (at least 70 per cent cocoa solids), chopped into small pieces

300ml double cream

grated chocolate or sprinkles, to decorate (optional)

Preheat the oven to 180°C/gas mark 4 and lightly grease a 20cm round cake tin.

Place the hazelnuts and stevia in a food processer and process together until finely ground.

In a bowl, whisk the egg whites until they form medium to stiff peaks. Fold in the hazelnut mix and stir well, but do not over-stir.

Spoon the cake mixture into the prepared tin and bake for 30–40 minutes.

To make the chocolate cream, gently heat the chocolate in a metal or glass bowl over a pan of gently simmering water. Be careful not to leave on the heat too long or get too hot, as chocolate splits very easily. Take it off the heat when it is nearly all melted (it will continue to melt when off the heat) and leave to cool slightly.

In a separate bowl, whisk the cream until it forms soft peaks, then fold in the melted chocolate. Stir well, and if it loosens up too much, pop it in the fridge until set and spreading consistency.

When you're ready to go, cut the cake in half horizontally. Spread a layer of chocolate cream over the bottom half, then top with the other half. Finish with another layer of cream on top, and decorate with grated chocolate or sprinkles, if you like.

NIBBLES

Cocoa, cinnamon and vanilla-roasted macadamias

✱✶✶ *Although nuts are usually a savoury snack, here I've decided to sweeten them up a little. These satisfy any sugary craving, but are very low in carbs.*

616 ENERGY KJ	149 ENERGY KCAL	2.2g PROTEIN	15g FAT	2.3g SATURATED FAT	1.1g CARBOHYDRATES	0.8g TOTAL SUGARS	01.2g FIBRE	0.2g SALT

SERVES 8 AS A SNACK

1 tablespoon cocoa powder

1 tablespoon stevia

1 teaspoon ground cinnamon

1 teaspoon vanilla extract

150g macadamia nuts

1 free-range egg white, beaten

Preheat the oven to 160°C/gas mark 3 and line a baking sheet with greaseproof paper.

In a bowl, mix together the cocoa, stevia, cinnamon and vanilla extract. Stir in the macadamias to coat, then mix in the egg white.

Arrange in a single layer on the prepared baking sheet and roast for 15 minutes. Leave to cool before serving. These will keep for about 2 weeks in an airtight container.

Peanut and chilli hummus

✱✶✶ *Hummus is pretty essential in my house. It does contain carbs, but they are complex. I love serving this with pieces of veggies to dunk. This version contains peanuts and chilli for a satay-inspired twist on traditional hummus. It really is moreish.*

804 ENERGY KJ	193 ENERGY KCAL	7.1g PROTEIN	14.2g FAT	2.2g SATURATED FAT	9.9g CARBOHYDRATES	1.1g TOTAL SUGARS	3g FIBRE	0.6g SALT

SERVES 6–8

400g can chickpeas, drained

100g peanuts

1 garlic clove

1 teaspoon tahini

1 teaspoon sriracha chili

50ml light olive oil

juice of 2 lemons

salt and freshly ground pepper

Place all the ingredients in a food processor with 100ml water. Blitz until the mixture reaches your desired consistency and season to taste.

Serve with cucumber, carrots and celery sticks.

Parmesan chunks with truffle honey

★☆☆ *This is a perfect way to start an evening. Use the best Parmesan you can afford, and serve with a glass of Champagne.*

183 ENERGY KJ ┊ 44 ENERGY KCAL ┊ 3.6g PROTEIN ┊ 3g FAT ┊ 1.9g SATURATED FAT ┊ 0.7g CARBOHYDRATES ┊ 0.7g TOTAL SUGARS ┊ 0g FIBRE ┊ 0.2g SALT

SERVES 10

1 teaspoon truffle honey

100g aged Parmesan cheese, cut into
    large chunks

Very simple – drizzle the truffle honey over the Parmesan chunks, and enjoy.

Wasabi tuna tartare in cucumber cups

★★☆ *I love these canapés – they are so simple, so full of flavour and so healthy. They look gorgeous, too. Try and get the freshest tuna possible, as obviously there is no cooking involved. These are possibly my healthiest canapes to date, so are great if you are wanting to graze without adding too many calories.*

59 ENERGY KJ ┊ 14 ENERGY KCAL ┊ 2.2g PROTEIN ┊ 0.5g FAT ┊ 0.1g SATURATED FAT ┊ 0.2g CARBOHYDRATES ┊ 0.1g TOTAL SUGARS ┊ 0.1g FIBRE ┊ 0.1g SALT

MAKES ABOUT 24

½ teaspoon wasabi

2 teaspoons soy sauce

2cm piece of fresh ginger, finely
    grated

dash of sesame oil

3 spring onions, finely sliced

1 cucumber

200g very fresh tuna loin, diced

1 red chilli, deseeded and chopped
    into tiny batons

1 tablespoon wasabi tobiko

In a small bowl, mix together the wasabi, soy, ginger, sesame oil and spring onions. Set aside.

Peel the cucumber and slice it into 3–4cm slices. Using a teaspoon, make a very small indentation in each slice. Lay the slices out on a sheet of clean kitchen paper until needed.

When you are ready to go, mix the tuna with the wasabi and soy dressing, then spoon it into the little cucumber cups. Top each one with a little sliver of chilli and a spoonful of tobiko, and serve.

Chicken liver parfait and red onion marmalade on chicken skin

✖✖✖ *These little babies are brilliant: you get a double whammy of chicken flavour, the crunch of the chicken, the smoothness and richness of pâté and a hint of sweetness. Personally, it's my perfect canapé. Recently I entered it into a competition and it got Marcus Wareing's special recommendation. Marcus is one of my favourite chefs, so I was super chuffed.*

400 ENERGY KJ	97 ENERGY KCAL	2.4g PROTEIN	8.4g FAT	3.6g SATURATED FAT	2.8g CARBOHYDRATES	2.6g TOTAL SUGARS	0.1g FIBRE	0.2g SALT

MAKES 20

250g chicken skin

100g red onion marmalade

salt and freshly ground black pepper

small edible flowers, to garnish

For the Chicken liver parfait

50g unsalted butter

1 large shallot, finely chopped

1 garlic clove, crushed

150g free-range chicken livers, trimmed

15ml brandy

100ml double cream

2 sprigs of thyme, leaves picked and finely chopped

½ tablespoon sea salt

a pinch of freshly ground black pepper

Preheat the oven to 180°C/gas mark 4. Take two baking trays that fit snugly on top of each other and cut two sheets of greaseproof paper to fit the trays. Line one of the trays with one of the sheets. Take the chicken skin and lay it out on top of the paper, spreading it out flat. Season with salt and pepper. Top with the other sheet of greaseproof paper, then fit the second baking tray on top. Bake for 30 minutes until golden and crisp, then leave to cool.

Now make the chicken liver parfait. Place a large frying pan over a medium heat and add the butter. Let it melt, then add the shallots and garlic and cook for about 8 minutes until translucent.

Add the chicken livers and continue to cook for about 10 minutes, turning frequently, until they are golden and brown. Add the brandy, cook off the alcohol and then add the cream and the thyme. Add the salt and pepper, then take off the heat.

Leave the mixture to cool slightly, then transfer to a blender and blitz until very smooth. Place in a bowl and cover in clingfilm, with the clingfilm pressed down on top of the parfait so that it doesn't develop a skin. Leave to cool completely, then, either in a blender or by hand, beat again. Transfer to a piping bag.

Break the chicken skin into small cracker-sized shapes. Pipe a little parfait on top of each one, then add a bit of red onion marmalade. Arrange on a serving plate and garnish with small edible flowers.

Goat's cheese and truffle mousse on beetroot crisps

* * * *This is a great low-carb canapé, and it looks great, too. The beetroot crisps resemble little petals.*

182 ENERGY KJ	44 ENERGY KCAL	2.7g PROTEIN	3.6g FAT	2.3g SATURATED FAT	0.5g CARBOHYDRATES	0.5g TOTAL SUGARS	0.1g FIBRE	0.3g SALT

MAKES ABOUT 20

vegetable oil, for frying

4 medium beetroots, peeled and very
    thinly sliced

250g fresh rindless goat's cheese

1 teaspoon chopped truffle

1 teaspoon truffle oil

salt and freshly ground black pepper

Heat about 2cm of vegetable oil in a saucepan over a medium heat. When it's hot, fry the beetroot slices off, in batches, for 2–3 minutes until crisp. Remove from the pan with a slotted spoon and drain on kitchen paper.

Use a whisk or hand blender to whip up the goat's cheese in a bowl with the chopped truffle and truffle oil. Season with salt and pepper and transfer to a piping bag. Pipe the mousse onto the beetroot crisps and serve.

Parmesan crisps

* * * *You might find that the low-carb approach leaves you craving that savoury crunch experience. These Parmesan crisps satisfy those needs, but without the carbs.*

347 ENERGY KJ	83 ENERGY KCAL	7.2g PROTEIN	5.9g FAT	3.9g SATURATED FAT	0.2g CARBOHYDRATES	0.2g TOTAL SUGARS	0g FIBRE	0.4g SALT

MAKES ABOUT 20

400g Parmesan cheese, grated

4 sprigs of rosemary, leaves picked

Preheat the oven to 160°C/gas mark 3 and line a baking sheet with greaseproof paper.

Sprinkle the cheese in an even layer across the tray. Sprinkle the rosemary leaves over the top. Pop in the oven for 15 minutes, or until melted and golden brown.

Remove from the oven and leave to cool, then break into pieces and enjoy. The crisps will keep for about 1 week in an airtight container.

Spiced soy seaweed crisps

★☆☆ *When I was a kid, my mother would give me toasted nori seaweed sheets as a snack when all I really wanted was jam sandwiches. It certainly made me stand out at school when we all compared our packed lunches, though! I now buy masses of the stuff, ready-toasted and spicy from Asian supermarkets in Chinatown, but these often contain monosodium glutamate, which I don't want. So here is a good homemade version that has the crunch factor and umami hit I desire. It's full of nutrients, too.*

289 ENERGY KJ	69 ENERGY KCAL	3.8g PROTEIN	3.7g FAT	0g SATURATED FAT	7.1g CARBOHYDRATES	6.9g TOTAL SUGARS	4.4g FIBRE	2.1g SALT

SERVES 4

½ tablespoon sesame oil

½ teaspoon grated fresh ginger

1 teaspoon runny honey

½ teaspoon chilli powder

50ml soy sauce

1 packet nori seaweed sheets

Preheat the oven to 150°C/gas mark 2. Line a baking sheet with greaseproof paper. You may need two baking sheets, depending on their size.

In a bowl, mix together the sesame oil, ginger, honey, chilli powder and soy sauce.

Brush this mixture onto one side of the nori seaweed sheets and then lay them out in a single layer on the prepared baking sheet[s].

Bake for 15–20 minutes until crispy, then remove from the oven. Leave to cool, then break them up into bite-size pieces. These will keep in an airtight container for a few days.

Chef's Tip: *If you prefer, you can slow cook these crisps overnight at 60°C.*

MARINADES

When you are dieting, you sometimes just want something quick that's easy to remember and execute. If you don't have the time for one of the more involved recipes, you might opt to go for a simple grilled chicken breast or steak with some veggies. If you go down that route, try using the marinades or spice rubs below. They are easy and speedy, but add a really good flavour, transforming a plain piece of meat into something special.

✱✫✫ Jerk marinade

Per 100g — 752 ENERGY KJ | 181 ENERGY KCAL | 2.2g PROTEIN | 14.5g FAT | 2.1g SATURATED FAT | 12.8g CARBOHYDRATES | 10.9g TOTAL SUGARS | 0.6g FIBRE | 0.1g SALT

1 teaspoon ground allspice

1 teaspoon pink peppercorns

½ teaspoon dried chilli flakes

1 tablespoon runny honey

50ml pineapple juice

small bunch of fresh coriander

4 garlic cloves

5cm piece of fresh ginger

1 Scotch bonnet chilli pepper

25ml olive oil

Place all the ingredients in a food processor and blitz until smooth. Rub into the meat before cooking. There's no real time limit on how long you have to marinate for, but remember, the longer you do so, the more flavour you get.

✱✫✫ Greek marinade

Per 100g — 1822 ENERGY KJ | 442 ENERGY KCAL | 2.5g PROTEIN | 44.7g FAT | 6.4g SATURATED FAT | 6.4g CARBOHYDRATES | 1.7g TOTAL SUGARS | 1g FIBRE | 0.1g SALT

zest and juice of 1 lemon

1 teaspoon dried chilli flakes

4 garlic cloves, finely chopped

1 teaspoon dried oregano

25ml white wine

50ml olive oil

Mix the ingredients together in a bowl. Rub into the meat before cooking. As before, the longer you marinate, the bigger the flavour.

✱✫✫ Thai marinade

Per 100g — 755 ENERGY KJ | 182 ENERGY KCAL | 3.3g PROTEIN | 14.5g FAT | 12.3g SATURATED FAT | 10.9g CARBOHYDRATES | 7.3g TOTAL SUGARS | 0.7g FIBRE | 0.8g SALT

5cm piece of fresh ginger, peeled

1 red chilli

zest of 1 lime

1 lemongrass stalk

½ teaspoon ground turmeric

2 garlic cloves, peeled

1 shallot, peeled

50ml coconut cream

1 teaspoon sugar

1 teaspoon fish sauce

Place all the ingredients in a food processor and blitz until smooth. Rub into the meat before cooking.

✱✫✫ Barbecue spice mix

Per 30g — 304 ENERGY KJ | 74 ENERGY KCAL | 3.3g PROTEIN | 2.5g FAT | 0.4g SATURATED FAT | 11.7g CARBOHYDRATES | 4.3g TOTAL SUGARS | 0.5g FIBRE | 3g SALT

1½ teaspoons smoked paprika

1 teaspoon dried garlic powder

½ teaspoon dried oregano

½ teaspoon ground cumin

1 teaspoon brown sugar

1 teaspoon cayenne pepper

1 teaspoon celery salt

Mix all the ingredients together well in a bowl. Rub into the meat before cooking.

Greek marinade
I love using this marinade for chicken thighs, lamb and fish.

Jerk marinade
Makes enough to marinate a whole chicken. Works really well with pork and fish.

Thai marinade
This is good on everything! Try it on tofu or prawns.

Barbecue spice mix
This is great on ribs or pulled pork.

DRESSINGS AND SAUCES

Yuzu dressing

✱✱✱ *Yuzu is a bit 'trendy', but don't be put off – it has a truly unique flavour. It is basically a miniature Japanese lime and tastes like pink grapefruit, bergamot and lime. It's very aromatic. You can buy the juice bottled online or in Asian supermarkets in little bottles.*

Per 100g

52 ENERGY KJ	12 ENERGY KCAL	0.4g PROTEIN	0.1g FAT	0g SATURATED FAT	2.7g CARBOHYDRATES	2.4g TOTAL SUGARS	0.1g FIBRE	0g SALT

MAKES ABOUT 15 SERVINGS

150ml lime juice

150ml lemon juice

50ml yuzu juice

5cm piece of fresh ginger, finely
    grated

1 teaspoon Tabasco green jalapeño
    sauce

Simply mix all of the ingredients together in a bowl. Any that you don't use now will keep for a few weeks in the fridge.

Truffle dressing

✱✱✱ *A lot of chefs turn their noses up at truffle oil, but I like it. Ideally I would like to use fresh white truffles, but I don't have the budget for that, so this suits me fine. A little goes a long way and I enjoy the heady aroma. This dressing is earthy, sexy and works well on hearty salads: think lentils, peas and broad beans, grilled beef and endive, french beans and foie gras... that sort of vibe.*

Per 30g

701 ENERGY KJ	170 ENERGY KCAL	0.1g PROTEIN	18.5g FAT	2.6g SATURATED FAT	0.4g CARBOHYDRATES	0.4g TOTAL SUGARS	0g FIBRE	0.1g SALT

MAKES 10 SERVINGS

250ml good-quality Chardonnay
    white wine vinegar

375ml extra virgin olive oil

50ml truffle oil

1 tablespoon Dijon mustard

1 teaspoon runny honey

salt and freshly ground black pepper

Simply mix all of the ingredients together in a bowl. Any that you don't use now will keep for a few weeks in the fridge.

Gluten- and sugar-free mustard

★★☆ *I found it something of a revelation when I first made mustard at home. I didn't realise how easy it was, and it makes such a difference. This is a plain mustard with limited sugar, but it would be great with some spices, honey or with different vinegars.*

Per 100g

59 ENERGY KJ	15 ENERGY KCAL	8.5g PROTEIN	9.6g FAT	0.5g SATURATED FAT	0.4g CARBOHYDRATES	0.4g TOTAL SUGARS	0g FIBRE	0.5g SALT

MAKES 1 350ML JAR

100g yellow mustard seeds

50g black mustard seeds

300ml cider vinegar

½ teaspoon salt

small pinch of ground allspice

Mix all the mustard seeds together in a bowl and then pour over the vinegar. Cover with clingfilm and leave overnight.

The next day, add the salt and allspice. Transfer half of the mixture to a food processor and blitz to form a paste. Mix this back into the bowl with the other half of the mixture.

Spoon into a sterilised jar (see page 184) and leave for a week for the flavour to mature. Then use!

Low-sugar tomato ketchup

★☆☆ *I love ketchup. I mean sadly, truly, deeply love it, in a very non-cheffy way. It's usually full of sugar, though, and that makes it a no-no during this diet. In this recipe, I have been very strict and only used sweetener, but if I wasn't feeling too strict I would add a tablespoon of maple syrup, too. It really is good, and perks up brekkie no end.*

Per 100g

234 ENERGY KJ	56 ENERGY KCAL	3.2g PROTEIN	0.5g FAT	0g SATURATED FAT	8.4g CARBOHYDRATES	8.2g TOTAL SUGARS	1.6g FIBRE	0.9g SALT

MAKES 1 350ML JAR

200g tomato purée

150ml cider vinegar

1 teaspoon mustard powder

1 tablespoon stevia

pinch of ground allspice

½ teaspoon celery salt

dash of Worcestershire sauce

Mix together all the ingredients in a small saucepan with 100ml water. Place over a medium heat and bring to the boil, then reduce the heat and simmer for about 10 minutes. Remove from the heat and leave to cool.

Spoon into a sterilised jar (see page 184) and seal.

FIVE WAYS WITH PICKLES

Pickles make a brilliant snack when you're dieting, and also add crunch, texture and flavour to many dishes. Sugar is often used when making pickles, but other sweeteners work well, too. I have used different aromatics with each one, but you don't need to include these if you don't have them – the vinegar, sweetener and salt are the important elements.

Sterilising jars

This is really very easy.

Simply wash the jars out with hot soapy water and make sure you have rubbed and scraped off any labels. Rinse off all the residue, but don't worry about drying them – they will dry in the oven. Place the jars in a preheated oven at 140°C/gas mark 1 for 20 minutes.

Keep in a warm oven until you are ready to fill.

★★☆ Pickled fennel

Per 100g

69 ENERGY KJ	17 ENERGY KCAL	0.9g PROTEIN	0.2g FAT	0g SATURATED FAT	1.7g CARBOHYDRATES	1.4g TOTAL SUGARS	1.8g FIBRE	0.8g SALT

MAKES 2 350ML JARS
150ml white wine vinegar
1 large piece of orange rind
1 teaspoon sea salt
1 star anise
2 tablespoons stevia
2 medium fennel bulbs, core
   removed, cut into thin strips
2 garlic cloves, peeled
1 red chilli, halved lengthways

Pour the vinegar into a saucepan with 50ml water and place over a medium heat.

Add the orange rind, salt, star anise and stevia to the vinegar mix and bring to the boil. Reduce the heat and simmer for 2 minutes, then take it off the heat.

Divide the fennel between two sterilised jars (see above), along with the garlic and chilli. Pour over the vinegar mix. Leave to cool, then seal the jars and place in the fridge. Leave for about 24 hours, then enjoy as a snack or with cheese and hams.

★★☆ Pickled honey beets

Per 100g

148 ENERGY KJ	35 ENERGY KCAL	1.3g PROTEIN	0.3g FAT	0g SATURATED FAT	6.2g CARBOHYDRATES	5.9g TOTAL SUGARS	1.1g FIBRE	1.3g SALT

MAKES 2 350ML JARS

6–8 medium raw beetroots

150ml cider vinegar

1 teaspoon salt

1 tablespoon runny honey

1 teaspoon dried chilli flakes

Place the beetroots in a saucepan and cover with water. Bring to the boil, then reduce the heat and simmer for 30 minutes. When cooked, take off the heat, drain and run under cold water. Now, using your hands (wear gloves if you don't want pink palms!), rub off the skins. Finally, slice the beetroots and layer up in 2 sterilised jars (see page 184).

Place the vinegar, salt, honey and chilli flakes in a pan with 50ml water over a high heat. Bring to the boil and then simmer for 2 minutes. Take off the heat.

Leave the vinegar mix to cool slightly, then pour over the beetroots. Seal the jars and leave for 24 hours before eating.

★★☆ Pickled onion slices

Per 100g

159 ENERGY KJ	38 ENERGY KCAL	1g PROTEIN	0.3g FAT	0g SATURATED FAT	7.2g CARBOHYDRATES	5.9g TOTAL SUGARS	0.8g FIBRE	1g SALT

MAKES 1 350ML JAR

4 medium onions, sliced into
    1cm rings

2 tablespoons sea salt

400ml malt vinegar

2 tablespoons runny honey

1 tablespoon stevia

1 teaspoon dried chilli flakes

1 teaspoon yellow mustard seeds

Place the onions in a bowl and sprinkle over the salt, then leave overnight at room temperature.

The next day, rinse off the salt and pat the onion slices dry with kitchen paper.

Place the vinegar, honey, stevia, chilli flakes and mustard seeds in a saucepan over a high heat. Bring to the boil and then simmer for a couple of minutes. Take off the heat and leave to cool.

Layer up the onions slices in a sterilised jar (see page 184), then pour over the cooled vinegar mixture. Seal and leave for a couple of weeks for the best pickle.

★★☆ Pickled celeriac with mustard seeds

Per 100g

78 ENERGY KJ	19 ENERGY KCAL	1g PROTEIN	0.4g FAT	0g SATURATED FAT	1.6g CARBOHYDRATES	1.3g TOTAL SUGARS	2.3g FIBRE	0.8g SALT

MAKES 2 350ML JARS

300ml white wine vinegar

2 tablespoons stevia

1 teaspoon sea salt

1 teaspoon yellow mustard seeds

1 large celeriac, peeled and cut
    into batons

Pour the vinegar into a saucepan with 50ml water over a high heat. Add the stevia, salt and mustard seeds. Bring to the boil and then simmer for 2 minutes. Take off the heat and leave to cool.

Divide the celeriac between two sterilised jars (see page 184) and pour over the vinegar mixture. Seal the jars and then place in a cool place for 24 hours before eating.

★★☆ Low-sugar dill pickles

Per 100g

56 ENERGY KJ	14 ENERGY KCAL	0.9g PROTEIN	0.3g FAT	0g SATURATED FAT	1.3g CARBOHYDRATES	1.1g TOTAL SUGARS	0.4g FIBRE	0.7g SALT

MAKES 2 350ML JARS

about 15 Lebanese cucumbers,
    topped and tailed and cut
    lengthways into quarters (you
    can use baby cucumbers if you
    can't get Lebanese)

500ml white wine vinegar

1 tablespoon stevia

1 teaspoon yellow mustard seeds

pinch of dried chilli flakes

1 tablespoon sea salt

4 garlic cloves

a small handful each of fresh
    tarragon and dill

Place the vinegar, stevia, mustard seeds, chilli flakes and salt in a saucepan with 50ml water over a high heat. Bring to the boil and then simmer for 2 minutes. Take off the heat and leave to cool.

Squash the garlic cloves and divide between two sterilised jars (see page 184). Add the cucumbers and herbs to the jars, then pour over the cooled vinegar mix.

Seal the jars and leave in a cool place for a few days before eating.

[Pictured below, top] *Pickled celeriac with mustard seeds* (page 186) and [bottom] *Pickled honey beets* (page 185)

Low-sugar dill pickles (page 186)

Pickled fennel (page 184)

Planning your meals

Starting a new diet can be daunting, so I recommend you plan your meals with care, especially at first, to make sure that everything you eat fits in with the plan. I've created two sample weekly meal plans below. Some of the meals I have used are not full recipes from this book, but are simple meals that you can create yourself. This is just to show you how easy it is to adapt the diet to suit your lifestyle.

	BREAKFAST	LUNCH	DINNER
Monday	Avocado, mint and white grape smoothie (page 14)and Bircher muesli (page 28)	Roast beef, red onion, roasted squash and blue cheese radicchio wraps (page 72) – using leftovers from Sunday's roast	Cod with braised fennel and cockle dressing (page 132)
Tuesday	Green eggs with quinoa (page 49) – using leftover broccoli from Sunday lunch	Kale and turkey superfood salad with miso soy dressing (page 76)	Spring lamb, pea and broad bean casserole (page 120) with Sweet, slow-cooked olive oil, garlic and lemon courgettes (page 144)
Wednesday	Creamy goat's cheese and herb omelette (page 43)	Chicken, hummus, sriracha and avocado wraps (page 72)	Chargrilled prawns with ouzo butter (page 134) and Asparagus with bottarga butter (page 144)
Thursday	Popeye juice (page 18) and Baked macadamia, pistachio and sour cherry granola (page 29)	Summer chopped salad (page 68)	Grilled steak and Braised spring vegetables (page 154)
Friday	Truffle and Parmesan scrambled eggs with Parma ham (page 52)	Dorset crab and white asparagus with white balsamic and honey dressing (page 94)	Moussaka-stuffed aubergine (page 113)
Saturday	Big Sur eggs benedict (page 46)	Chicken paillard with honey, chilli and fennel marinade (page 102)	Low-carb dim sum (pages 108–109)
Sunday	Sunshine juice (page 17) and Huevos rancheros (page 45)	Oysters grilled with Lardo (page 122) (starter), followed by Roast beef, celeriac gratin, wild mushrooms and charred onions (pages 116–117)	Honey- and mustard-glazed gammon with Waldorf slaw (page 112)

Index